D0961082

ACCLAIM FOR
The Hell with Love

"Witty and wise."
—*People*

"Sassy. Certain to improve your spirits
and repair your battered ego."
—*Hartford Courant*

"The greatest anthology of poetry I have
ever read. . . . It reminds me why I fell in
love with poetry in the first place."
—Andrew Carroll, director,
The American Poetry & Literacy Project

"I love this book . . . wise to the ways of the
heart. . . . Whether you've been heartbroken for
two hours or two months, splash cold water on
your face and go . . . buy this book."
—Matthew Klam,
author of *Sam the Cat*

"Expertly selected . . . an invaluable
companion to the lovelorn of all ages."
—Lucinda Rosenfeld,
author of *What She Saw*

"An invigorating anthology."
—*Denver Rocky Mountain News*

Also by Mary D. Esselman and Elizabeth Ash Vélez
The Hell with Love

Kiss Off

POEMS TO SET YOU FREE

Edited by
Mary D. Esselman
and Elizabeth Ash Vélez

WARNER BOOKS

An AOL Time Warner Company

Anna Akhmatova, "We Don't Know How to Say Goodbye," trans-
lated by Stanley Kunitz, from *Poems of Akhmatova*. Copyright 1973
by Stanley Kunitz and Max Hayward. Reprinted by permission of
Darhansoff and Verrill Literary Agency on behalf of Stanley Kunitz.

Copyright information continued on page 202

Warner Books, Inc., 1271 Avenue of the Americas,
New York, NY 10020

Visit our Web site at www.twbookmark.com.

 An AOL Time Warner Company

Printed in the United States of America

First Printing: January 2003
10 9 8 7 6 5 4 3 2 1

Library of Congress Control Number: 2002114051
ISBN: 0-446-69028-7 *2722   9474 3/03*

Book design and text composition by Ellen Gleeson
Cover design by Janet Perr

*This is dedicated to the ones we love:
our friends, our families, our students,
and our teachers.*

Contents

Contents

Dealing
WHEN YOU FACE FACTS

Contents

Healing

WHEN YOU FIND YOURSELF 123

Believing

WHEN YOU STAY STRONG

Introduction

Here's what we know for sure: Life will break your heart in a million different ways. And we don't just mean the heartbreak of losing the love of your life (although that definitely hurts). We mean nothing is as easy as you thought it would be. You were supposed to be a Supreme Court justice by now, happily married to a pediatric brain surgeon, proud mother of three kick-ass kids (all budding Rhodes scholars of course). Oh, and a really good cook, who grows her own vegetables.

But here you are, well past a certain age, and you still can't seem to meet a decent guy, you hate your idiot boss, and you wake up every morning asking yourself, "What's the f*?@!*ing point?"

How do you fix *this* kind of heartbreak, the kind that comes from losing faith in yourself and the world? And how do you figure out how to be the person you always dreamed you would be— tough but kind, honest but nobody's fool, smart but loving?

Some of us try to do that by finding a "role model" (like Catholic-girl Mary trying to be feminist theorist Elizabeth—who's trying to be grande dame Georgia O'Keefe). Others faithfully follow Dr. Phil, Dr. Laura, or Dr. Sarah Jessica Parker, thinking they'll find the secret to their authentic, morally centered, totally cutting-edge Jimmy Choo–shod selves. But we think that for direction and inspiration, nothing beats the power of poetry. So we put together a collection of poems to help you discover who you really are and guide you toward a life of joy and fulfillment.

Of course we know this is not as easy as it sounds—it's not "Take two Emily Dickinsons and call us in the morning." It's more like: Take stock of your life, kiss off everything that's holding you back from happiness, and start the long, hard process of deciding what you need and what you truly want.

Most of us have been doing this kind of soul-searching for years, trying to find some philosophical framework, religious structure, or daily routine that will help us shape our lives. And many of us have turned to our favorite literature for some articulation of (or escape from) the vague dissatisfaction we feel. And while we (Mary and Elizabeth) have often come across a poem that hits just the right spot at just the right moment, we haven't found a collection that matches the poem with the moment the way we'd like. That's what we've always wanted, a guidebook on how to live using poetry, with sections such as "How to Talk to Your Mother" or "Being Alone and Liking It." Wouldn't it be great, we've thought, if we had a sort of doctor's manual where you could just look up your ailment—broken heart, messed-up family, elusive vocation—and receive perfect poems to treat your pain?

That's the kind of book we attempted in *The Hell with Love*, a collection of literary therapy for the brokenhearted. We matched angry, despairing, hilarious poems with the various stages of heartbreak, like Rage, Sadness, or Real Hope. To our delight, the book found an audience—and not just with readers coming out of breakups or divorces. We heard from people dealing with death, illness, family struggles, and all kinds of loss. The poems offered a comfort they hadn't found elsewhere.

What really heartened us was when people told us they thought they hated poetry until they'd read our book. Putting the poems in the context of their feelings helped them "get" the meaning. Poetry no longer seemed like fancy gobbledygook to them—it was practical. Poetry was funny and naughty, stern and wise, like the best of best friends. That was one of our original goals—to get people reading poetry the way they read *People* magazine. What if people knew the 50 Most Beautiful Poems by heart, the way they know every last detail about the 50 Most Beautiful People?

So we decided to bring out a new book of literary therapy, full of more poetry that we love. *Kiss Off: Poems to Set You Free* isn't just for the newly jilted, it's for anyone suffering from loss, disappointment, or that general Hamlet-ish feeling every morning that something is rotten in Denmark. In other words, it's for everyone trying to find their way back to happiness. *Kiss Off* moves from poems that express loneliness and frustration, to poems that show how we hide or run from unhappiness, to poems about hard-won self-awareness, and finally to poems of acceptance and joy. And to help people relate the poems to their own lives, we provide commentary for each section.

Despite our titles, *The Hell with Love* and *Kiss Off,* we're not angry women writers. We love love! We love the world! It's just coincidence (really) that the title of our second book comes from one of our favorite songs by . . . well, by the Violent Femmes. It's called "Kiss Off," and it sums up just about all the reasons we think people feel so bereft—and why they need poetry (or good lyrics) to help them through:

> *I take one one one 'cause you left me and*
> *two two two for my family and*
> *3 3 3 for my heartache and*
> *4 4 4 for my headaches and*
> *5 5 5 for my lonely and*
> *6 6 6 for my sorrow and*

7 7 for no tomorrow and
8 8 I forget what 8 was for and
9 9 9 for a lost god and
10 10 10 10 for everything
everything everything everything

We believe that really great poetry can help set you free from "everything everything everything." It helps articulate what you're feeling, lets you recognize yourself in someone else's words, creates form out of your chaos, and offers you hope. And poetry is compact and portable, but rich with meaning—it's like having a cell phone with a direct line to the Dalai Lama.

Poet Laureate Billy Collins says, "In times of crisis it's interesting that people don't turn to the novel or say, 'We should all go out to a movie,' or 'Ballet would help us.' It's always poetry. What we want to hear is a human voice speaking directly in our ear."* And poet Deborah Garrison notes, "In poetry there's the pure essence of life distilled

*Quoted in the *New York Times*, 10/01/01, "The Early Intimate Power of Poetry to Console," by Dinitia Smith.

in a few words, and its very distilled form gives people something to hang on to."*

We hope that you will find that pure, distilled essence in these poems, so that you'll learn to live with joy again. William Carlos Williams puts it best when he says:

> My heart rouses
>   thinking to bring you news
>   of something
> that concerns you
>   and concerns many men. Look at
>   what passes for new.
> You will not find it there but in
>   despised poems.
>   It is difficult
> to get the news from poems
>   yet men die miserably every day
>   for lack
> of what is found there.

---

*Quoted in the *New York Times*, 11/1/01, "Poetic History of the Heart," by Martin Arnold.

Hurting

WHEN THINGS FALL APART

One day, it just happens. You completely snap. Your last single friend announces her engagement to the schmo she met two months ago, or your married boss hits on you just when you think you've managed to impress him with your work smarts, or you're forced off the sidewalk by a J.Crew couple and their double-barreled baby stroller. It's all too much. It might not be dramatic—a sudden freak-out or breakdown. It could simply be the cumulative effect of watching the world surge past and around you—the showers, the weddings, the new houses, the better jobs, the damn baby photos. Everyone else seems to know what she wants—and how to get it—yet you consistently feel overlooked, underloved, and, let's face it, screwed, in every way except literally.

You know you shouldn't feel this way. You don't want to become some whiney malcontent.

But you can't shake this unresolved restlessness, this nameless dissatisfaction with your life. You've tried to put it in perspective—there's real tragedy in the world, real crisis and pain—you know, you know, you know. You know Fran the receptionist still aches for her husband, dead ten years, and you watched your friend Meg fight a brutal, losing battle with cancer. You've seen what illness and death and estrangement can do. You carry all sorts of loss within you.

That's why the baby stroller people or the smarmy boss or the schmo-marrying friend put you right over the edge—you're tired of losing people and losing hope. You feel a great longing for companionship and connectedness, for knowing that what you do means something, for gratification and peace of mind, but it keeps eluding you despite your best efforts. And every reminder of this longing cuts into your spirit again and again until you just can't take it. When will you stop feeling so bereft, mourning what you've lost (friends, true loves, your mother's approval) and what you've never had (the little household of your dreams, a soul-fulfilling vocation, your mother's approval)?

One way to start feeling better is to give your-self permission to kick and wail and grieve. Let the poets in Hurting help you express all of it—the rage, the despair, the what-am-I-doing-with-my-life agony. Think of this section as one big scream of frustration. All we know is that we just feel pain, the kind that comes from being scraped in the same place over and over again. Like the speaker in Lola Haskins's "Love," we're raw with feeling, oversensitized to everything that's ever hurt us. We don't know quite what's hit us, we just feel our skin's been ripped off.

But deep down, we really *do* know what's hit us—crushing disappointment after disappoint-ment. Some big (your parents were supposed to stay together forever), some small (that cellulite was supposed to disappear after you went off the Pill), and some that we try to say are small when we know they're really big (we were supposed to have snagged The One, flex-timed The Job, and delivered The Kids before The Fertility Plunge). Tack on general injustice, poverty, and terror, and you feel too bruised to bear it.

What gets us is the "why" of it all. Why us?

Did we ask for any of this? Weren't we entitled to something else? The speaker in Dorothy Parker's ironically named "Fulfillment" seems incredulous that this kind of pain is her reward for becoming a reasonably well-raised adult. "For this my mother wrapped me warm . . . And gave me roughage in my diet"? she asks. All so I could "grow to womanhood" and "break my heart to clattering bits"?

Talk about roughage in the diet—when you feel this forsaken, every disappointment seems too tough to digest. And we make matters worse by chewing each one to death! Somehow, perversely, we feed our own despair. We keep careful track of every little thing that has hurt us, we nurse our grudges, we stay in the very situations that bring us down.

Look at the lovers in Anna Akhmatova's "We Don't Know How to Say Goodbye." The two of them are a picture of gloom—he's moody, she's his shadow, and they're sitting on a frozen branch in a graveyard outside a church where masses for the dead are being said. Not exactly a Harlequin romance! So why are they still together? If she wants to stop feeling "so different from the rest"—

if, like a lot of women we know, she wants a sunny bungalow of family happiness—then why is she willing to settle for his stick picture of a mansion in the snow? Why can't she find a way to say goodbye?

Maybe it's because she can't conceive of any identity for herself outside of him. Maybe it's because some relationships are just too difficult to sever—you can't just cut your father or your boss out of your life, no matter how "moody" (try "abusive") they are, can you? Or your oldest friend? Sometimes staying stuck in misery seems easier than razing your old life and building a new one.

Perhaps that's why the woman in Deborah Garrison's "Worked Late on a Tuesday Night" is alone and forlorn in the deserted streets, trying with no success to hail a cab home. This is not the first time she's been here, cold but "too stubborn to reach/into [her] pocket for a glove." Seems she's too stubborn to reach, period. For protection from the cold or for a better life than what she's got. She knows she's "not half/of what [she] meant to be," so why doesn't she change her life instead of just "cursing/the freezing rain"?

Why? Because of a little thing called pride.

Who wants to admit, "My life is a disaster, and every little part of me feels broken!"? We made the choices that led us here. We never meant to be alone and heartsick, but we did choose this job, this city, these relationships. We thought we were building a life for ourselves; now we're supposed to realize that instead we were slowly crumbling inside, helping along the decay of our ovaries and the dilapidation of our souls, à la Emily Dickinson's "Crumbling Is Not an Instant's Act"? That's outrageous and unfair and infuriating. How could we have known it would all work out this way? What should we have done differently?

And even if you do swallow your pride, even if you do admit you feel used up and useless, like the gum-decayed mother in Elizabeth Ash Vélez's "Thursday, 11:00 A.M.," or smushy and rotten like a pear spoiled "from the inside out" in Jane Kenyon's "The Pear"—then what? You're supposed to have the strength and wherewithal to just chuck everything and start over?: "Okay, this life sucks, so hmmm, I know what I'll do—I'll just quit my job and move somewhere perfect and do something much better, never mind that I haven't a clue where to go, what to do, or how to pay for any of it! Yippee, it's a plan!"

Not likely. At this point in Hurting all we know is that we've had enough, and we're too defensive and confused to do much about it. So instead of radically changing the big things in our lives, we usually opt for making last-ditch efforts to change the superficial things. Maybe if we tightened our torso, we'd feel more in control, so it's off to Pilates class. Maybe if those frown lines disappeared, we'd feel less anxious, so it's off to the BOTOX doc. Like the girlchild in Marge Piercy's "Barbie Doll," we run "to and fro apologizing" to ourselves for not being the person we always dreamed we'd be. As if we're offering one last desperate sacrifice to the God of Happiness, we cut off our noses to spite ourselves. There, I've done everything I can, we think. Now give me a better life!

And when no better life materializes, we truly fall into the kind of despair William Butler Yeats describes in "The Second Coming." We can't fix ourselves, we decide, because everything falls apart—our bodies, our lives, the world. No center holds anything together; it's all anarchy. So why bother trying to be the "beauty of the world, the paragon of animals," why bother trying to be some perfect Gap person in a shiny little Pottery Barn life? Like Hamlet, we tell ourselves there's no point. The world is nothing but a "foul and pestilent congregation of vapors," and we amount to nothing but a "quintessence of dust."

Okay, fine then, you think. I'll stop trying to please everyone else. I'll stop blaming myself for everything wrong in my life. I'll stop worrying about the misery of the world. Who needs any of it, anyway—the sea and trees, red ripe tomatoes, office blowhards, artsy posers? As poet Deborah Garrison eloquently says, "Fuck them all" ("Fight Song"). Or as poet Etheridge Knight more delicately puts it, "fuck/the whole mothafucking thing" ("Feeling Fucked Up").

So! Terrific! The Hurting poets have done such a good job of expressing all your sorrow and outrage that here you are feeling like a one big F-word piece of dust. This is supposed to make you feel better?

Well, we think it's a start—at least you're acknowledging your pain. It's real, and it hurts, and you're sick of it. The trick is how to move on from here.

What you don't want to do is stay trapped in this fuck-you frame of mind. If you isolate and alienate yourself from the world, you'll become the creature in Stephen Crane's "The Heart," squatting in a desert of your own making (like an angry loser on *Survivor*). Sure things were bad before when you were sitting in that cold grave-yard or being pelted by the freezing rain—but is this really an improvement? You've felt frustrated in your efforts to evolve into a fulfilled, happy person, but did you really mean to devolve into this—a naked, bestial monster eating its own bitter heart out?

Of course not. Ultimately what you want is what the speaker in Knight's poem is pining for—something and someone to love, so that "[your] soul can sing." Allow yourself to rant—fuck 'em all—but then get out of Hurting, fast. If you want to love life again, you'll need that heart of yours, and the less bitter, the better.

Love

She tries it on, like a dress.
She decides it doesn't fit,
and starts to take it off.
Her skin comes, too.

LOLA HASKINS

Fulfillment

For this my mother wrapped me warm,
And called me home against the storm,
And coaxed my infant nights to quiet,
And gave me roughage in my diet,
And tucked me in my bed at eight,
And clipped my hair, and marked my weight,
And watched me as I sat and stood:
That I might grow to womanhood
To hear a whistle and drop my wits
And break my heart to clattering bits.

DOROTHY PARKER

We Don't Know How to Say Goodbye

We don't know how to say goodbye,
We wander on, shoulder to shoulder
Already the sun is going down
You're moody, and I am your shadow.
Let's step inside a church, hear prayers,
    masses for the dead
Why are we so different from the rest?
Outside in the graveyard we sit on a
    frozen branch.

That stick in your hand is tracing
Mansions in the snow in which we will
    always be together.

ANNA AKHMATOVA
(Trans. Stanley Kunitz)

Worked Late
on a Tuesday Night

Again.
Midtown is blasted out and silent,
drained of the crowd and its doggy day.
I trample the scraps of deli lunches
some ate outdoors as they stared dumbly
or hooted at us career girls—the haggard
beauties, the vivid can-dos, open raincoats aflap
in the March wind as we crossed to and fro
in front of the Public Library

Never thought you'd be one of them,
did you, little lady?
Little Miss Phi Beta Kappa,
with your closetful of pleated
skirts, twenty-nine till death do us
part! Don't you see?
The good schoolgirl turns thirty,
forty, singing the song of time management
all day long, lugging the briefcase
home. So at 10:00 P.M.

you're standing here
with your hand in the air,

cold but too stubborn to reach
into your pocket for a glove, cursing
the freezing rain as though it were
your difficulty. It's pathetic,
and nobody's fault but
your own. Now

the tears,
down into the collar.
Cabs, cabs, but none for hire.
I haven't had dinner; I'm not half
of what I meant to be.
Among other things, the mother
of three. Too tired, tonight,
to seduce the father.

DEBORAH GARRISON

Crumbling Is Not an Instant's Act

Crumbling is not an instant's Act
   A fundamental pause
   Dilapidation's processes
   Are organized Decays.

'Tis first a Cobweb on the Soul
   A Cuticle of Dust
   A Borer in the Axis
   An Elemental Rust—

Ruin is formal—Devil's work
   Consecutive and slow—
Fail in an instant, no man did
   Slipping—is Crash's law.

EMILY DICKINSON

Thursday, 11:00 A.M.

At the periodontist,
I always read
what they have.
It says here:
mothers of adolescents
are often
pessimists
(wild with S.A.D.
and November light).
The book of
dental doom
suggests that
if I go on
as I have,
not flossing,
on aimless watch
for the spring,
I might easily
outlive my teeth.

ELIZABETH ASH VÉLEZ

The Pear

There is a moment in middle age
when you grow bored, angered
by your middling mind,
afraid.

That day the sun
burns hot and bright,
making you more desolate.

It happens subtly, as when a pear
spoils from the inside out,
and you may not be aware
until things have gone too far.

JANE KENYON

Barbie Doll

This girlchild was born as usual
and presented dolls that did pee-pee
and miniature GE stoves and irons
and wee lipsticks the color of cherry candy.
Then in the magic of puberty, a classmate said:
You have a great big nose and fat legs.

She was healthy, tested intelligent,
possessed strong arms and back,
abundant sexual drive and manual dexterity.
She went to and fro apologizing.
Everyone saw a fat nose on thick legs.

She was advised to play coy,
exhorted to come on hearty,
exercise, diet, smile and wheedle.
Her good nature wore out
like a fan belt.
So she cut off her nose and her legs
and offered them up.

In the casket displayed on satin she lay
with the undertaker's cosmetics painted on,
a turned-up putty nose,
dressed in a pink and white nightie.
Doesn't she look pretty? everyone said.
Consummation at last.
To every woman a happy ending.

MARGE PIERCY

The Second Coming

Turning and turning in the widening gyre
The falcon cannot hear the falconer;
Things fall apart; the centre cannot hold;
Mere anarchy is loosed upon the world,
The blood-dimmed tide is loosed,
    and everywhere
The ceremony of innocence is drowned;
The best lack all conviction, while the worst
Are full of passionate intensity.

Surely some revelation is at hand;
Surely the Second Coming is at hand.
The Second Coming! Hardly are those words out
When a vast image out of "Spiritus Mundi"
Troubles my sight: somewhere in sands
    of the desert
A shape with lion body and the head of a man,
A gaze blank and pitiless as the sun,
Is moving its slow thighs, while all about it
Reel shadows of the indignant desert birds.
The darkness drops again; but now I know

That twenty centuries of stony sleep
Were vexed to nightmare by a rocking cradle,
And what rough beast, its hour come round at last,
Slouches towards Bethlehem to be born?

WILLIAM BUTLER YEATS

Hamlet II.ii. 270–279

I have of late—but wherefore I know not—lost all my mirth, forgone all custom of exercises; and indeed it goes so heavily with my disposition that this goodly frame, the earth, seems to me a sterile promontory; this most excellent canopy, the air, look you, this brave o'erhanging firmament, this majestical roof fretted with golden fire, why, it appeareth nothing to me but a foul and pestilent congregation of vapors. What a piece of work is a man! How noble in reason, how infinite in faculties, in form and moving how express and admirable, in action how like an angel, in apprehension, how like a god! The beauty of the world, the paragon of animals! And yet, to me, what is this quintessence of dust?

WILLIAM SHAKESPEARE

Fight Song

Sometimes you have to say it:
Fuck them all.

Yes fuck them all—
the artsy posers,
the office blowhards
and brown-nosers;

Fuck the type who gets the job done
and the type who stands on principle;
the down-to-earth and understated;
the overhyped and underrated;

Project director?
Get a bullshit detector.

Client's mum?
Up your bum.

You can't be nice to everyone.

When your back is to the wall
When they don't return your call
When you're sick of saving face
When you're screwed in any case

Fuck culture scanners, contest winners,
subtle thinkers and the hacks who offend them;
people who give catered dinners
and (saddest of sinners) the sheep who attend
    them—

which is to say fuck yourself
and the person you were: polite and mature,
a trooper for good. The beauty is
they'll soon forget you

and if they don't
they probably should.

DEBORAH GARRISON

Feeling Fucked Up

Lord she's gone done left me done packed/up
    and split
and I with no way to make her
come back and everywhere the world is bare
bright bone white crystal sand glistens
dope death dead dying and jiving drove
her away made her take her laughter and her
    smiles
and her softness and her midnight sighs—

Fuck Coltrane and music and clouds drifting in
    the sky
fuck the sea and trees and the sky and birds
and alligators and all the animals that roam
    the earth

fuck marx and mao fuck fidel and nkrumah and
democracy and communism fuck smack and pot
and red ripe tomatoes fuck joseph fuck mary fuck
god jesus and all the disciples fuck fanon nixon
and malcolm fuck the revolution fuck freedom
    fuck
the whole muthafucking thing
all i want now is my woman back
so my soul can sing

ETHERIDGE KNIGHT

The Heart

In the desert
I saw a creature, naked, bestial,
Who, squatting upon the ground,
Held his heart in his hands,
And ate of it.

I said, "Is it good, friend?"
"It is bitter—bitter," he answered;
"But I like it
Because it is bitter,
And because it is my heart."

STEPHEN CRANE

Hiding
WHEN YOU SHUT DOWN

So you're miserably lonely and bitter, and you can't even believe this is who you've become—you never meant to end up Ms. Utterly Hurting. You always thought maybe you'd wind up more like Ms. Happily Ever After (post-feminist), some Lisa Simpson–meets-Madonna combination of smart little achiever turned sexy bad girl ruling the world turned married mom of two kids with cool names.

But no, here you are, wounded from disappointments you never imagined. All you know is you can't spend one more Thanksgiving with your fractured family, or one more year in your pressure-cooker cubicle, or one more decade losing people to death, distance, or domestic bliss (theirs, of course). You can't and you won't. You simply refuse to set yourself up for more let-downs, more pain.

So you hunker down tight in your little fortress, like Jodie Foster in *Panic Room*. You've got your Entire History of the Blues CDs, your two-year-old pile of unread *New Yorker* magazines, your collection of Thai take-out menus, your new interest in needlepoint—who needs family or friends when you've got all this to keep you happy, right? You put yourself in emotional storage—Rosie O'Donnell calls it "bubble-wrapping" your heart—until it's safe to come out again, if ever.

This is Hiding—when you pull back from the world, almost daring it to find you and hurt you again. You decline invitations, stop calling friends back, do the minimum at work (but always act tremendously busy)—in general, you push every-one away, halfway hoping they'll leave you alone in your misery, and halfway hoping they'll stick with you and somehow break the spell of your unhappi-ness. You're like the worst kind of adolescent—a sullen, door-slamming creature of darkness who secretly dreams of being Prom Queen.

In "Red Onion, Cherries, Boiling Potatoes,

Milk—," Jane Hirshfield warns us that when you become like this, "a soul, accepting nothing," you're in real danger of starving yourself. In Hiding we're like stubborn children, refusing everything, the delicious peaches as well as the nasty boiled potatoes and dry toast. We confuse sulking with "holding out for better." "No," we say, pursing our lips. No, we won't meet our friend-across-the-hall's-brother for drinks, and No, we won't join the office softball team. Too bad if that means we're saying no to the possibility of love or even just fun. Like the cut flowers that refuse to drink, we'd rather shrivel up and die than expose ourselves to the possibility of pain again.

But the heart sees what's really going on here, says Hirshfield. Even though we do our best to keep it at a great distance, the heart remains alert and tries to keep us from becoming like the speaker in Philip Larkin's "Wants," who desires only oblivion. Locked away in our safe rooms, we tell ourselves we're not missing a thing out there in the world. It's all a sham—invitation-cards to dull parties and other people's weddings, dinners, meetings, "the artful tensions of the calendar."

Who cares if Christmas is coming and then, relentlessly, New Year's Eve–and-no-date? Even sex seems to lack passion and intimacy; they're all just following "printed directions," or so you like to think, basing that generalization on your last long-ago experience with the seemingly attractive bicycle messenger. Everyone just pretends to be happy, they fake that pose of contentment in the family "photographed under the flagstaff." But *you* see all this for what it is—little activities to distract ourselves from the coming of death. You'd rather face it alone—hiding behind your triple-locked door, watching endless reruns of *Seinfeld*, teaching your cat to come when you call.

But deep down some part of you is still affected by beauty. You know that you are being childish and stubborn. You know that this lockdown is a conscious choice you are making. As Wang Wei suggests in "Returning to My Cottage," you still hear the "faraway bells echo in the valley." When you get up to open the window or change the channel, you hear laughter from your neighbor's dinner party, you hear doors opening and shutting as people come home and go out. The sky and the evening breeze still beckon to you. You consider calling up some friends and going out, but then the fear takes over. Why go out? Why try? You'll only be crushed again. A simple Wednesday evening begins to seem dark and somber, so you give up, "go in and bar the door."

Instead of being so hard on yourself because you're afraid to venture back into the world, maybe you just have to accept that this is what you feel like doing for the time being. You are like the speaker in Guillaume Apollinaire's "Hotel." You have checked in to a cage in your own heartbreak hotel, and even though the sun "puts his arm through the window," begging you to come out and play, you won't budge. In fact, you'll use the heat and warmth of the sun to light your self-destructive cigarette—"I don't want to work I want to smoke." You are filled with ennui and existential angst. And as the French philosophers suggest, perhaps for a while anyway, you *need* your cage, your own lonely space, your time to mend.

And as you pull back even further, you may begin to resent and fear the life around you. The sounds of life that penetrate your "shadowy upstairs bedroom" may not be reassuring. In "Summer: 6:00 A.M.," Jane Kenyon paints a picture of the neighbors that only confirms your decision to hide from the world. The mom next door is trapped by the defiant toddler and the unhappy infant, the older one wailing like a cicada. Meanwhile you hear her husband's footfalls, hard and deliberate, walking away from the house, leaving her with the kids and the beige, brown sameness of the day. So if this is marriage and motherhood, who needs it? you say. *You* can roll over and go back to sleep on your pristine, 300-thread Egyptian cotton sheets. You don't have to contend with screaming brats or sticky puddles of spilled juice. You belong to no one.

And if you happen to drag yourself out of your fortress and go for a quick walk around the neighborhood, your reflections on the natural world will confirm your decision to stay hidden away. In Larry Vélez's "Plainsong," a large loud raven comes across a sad remnant of human vanity, a discarded brown toupee (must belong to the pathetic bald guy across the street who's always yelling at his kids). You decide you'll be like the raven who "hasn't learned to want/what he doesn't need." You can stop wanting, you tell yourself. And then you notice the neighbor's unfinished skylight, and you are reminded of the wife's breakdown—she wanted too much (neighborhood gossips suggest that the stepfather was doing more than construction) and she paid for it. Even though it's spring, there's "death in careless abundance" out there in nature—and in human nature. Better to turn away from all of it, to play it safe, ask for less, want less, spend nothing.

Good luck, because guess what? You're doing what you set out *not* to do—setting yourself up for a big fall. How can you possibly be this superior being you've created in your head? You think you get to scoff at the way everyone else lives because only *you* know how to distance yourself from the messy spills and sad vanities of real life? Like the speaker in Richard Eberhart's "In a Hard Intellectual Light," you think you can outsmart life—you can build this citadel, beautiful and austere, that will protect you from the desire for closeness, tenderness, and intimacy. You will not give in to feeling. You will see everything only "in a hard intellectual light." But it won't work, Eberhart warns us—not only will we all have our fall, but our search for absolute perfection will kill all delight.

At this point, some part of us begins to understand that this hiding out, this "bubble-wrapping" of our hearts isn't working. Hiding is no longer any kind of refuge. You have tried to shut yourself away from pain and sorrow, but in the process you have also shut out joy and pleasure. You can barely taste the fifth or fifteenth Oreo, the air in your apartment is stale, and the Fiona Apple CD that you play over and over sounds like elevator music.

Jane Hirshfield, in "A Room," and Derek Walcott, in "The Fist," both show us that we are trying too hard. In "A Room," Hirshfield tells us that we cannot control what Eberhart calls our "body's soft jails," the weakness of the flesh. However desperately we want to deny our humanity and especially our feelings, we are still full of anger, grief, and, yes, desire. We do our best to become inanimate matter like the room that imprisons us, instructing our ribs each morning so that we will "neither respond nor draw back in fear," so that we will desire nothing. But to achieve this nothingness, you must clench yourself too tightly, like the fist that holds on to the heart in Walcott's "The Fist." Just hold on for one more day, you tell yourself. You try hard to ignore the brightness, the world with its pleasures and dangers. It's like learning to ride a bicycle. If you only concentrate on holding on, of course you'll fall.

The longer we continue to hide, the harder it becomes to ignore all the things we really want, like love and connection with others. We're holding on tightly to our defenses, but at the same time we desperately want to let go—as a result, we begin to develop "the strong/clench of the madman"—we start making ourselves a little crazy. Billy Collins's "Embrace" tells us to relax the grip, drop the pose, stop playing that goofy, seventh-grade parlor trick—the one where you pretend to be making out with someone when really it's just you with your arms wrapped around yourself. Do you really think you're fooling anyone, least of all yourself? You know that with your "crossed elbows and screwy grin" you have never looked so alone. If you don't start looking for a *real* embrace, if you don't release yourself from this restraint, you are not getting better. Instead, you have become your own straitjacket, locked in fear and bitterness, unable to move in any direction.

So free yourself from that loony bin. Stop hiding from all that's bad—and very good—in the world. Like the speaker in Louise Glück's "Mutable Earth," learn that you were wrong when you thought "if I had nothing/the world couldn't touch me." That safe room you created could never protect you anyway, because "the boundary, the wall/around the self erodes." Ultimately we realize that we weren't really *hiding*, we were waiting for our numbness to morph into hunger.

In the end, that hunger will drive us back into the world. Like the defiant child in Hirshfield's "Red Onion . . ." (she was waiting too) you will finally feel appetite. At last, you'll unbar the door, go lie in the new grass that greens the marshes, feel the evening breeze that "bends the water-rushes." And you'll feed your hungry heart.

Red Onion, Cherries, Boiling Potatoes, Milk—

Here is a soul, accepting nothing.
Obstinate as a small child
refusing tapioca, peaches, toast.

The cheeks are streaked, but dry.
The mouth is firmly closed in both directions.

Ask, if you like,
if it is merely sulking, or holding out for better.
The soup grows cold in the question.
The ice cream pools in its dish.

Not this, is all it knows. Not this.
As certain cut flowers refuse to drink in the vase.

And the heart, from its great distance, watches,
    helpless.

JANE HIRSHFIELD

Wants

Beyond all this, the wish to be alone:
However the sky grows dark with invitation-cards
However we follow the printed directions of sex
However the family is photographed under the
    flagstaff—
Beyond all this, the wish to be alone.

Beneath it all, desire of oblivion runs:
Despite the artful tensions of the calendar,
The life insurance, the tabled fertility rites,
The costly aversion of the eyes from death—
Beneath it all, desire of oblivion runs.

PHILIP LARKIN

Returning to My Cottage

Faraway bells echo in the valley
one by one the woodsmen are heading home.

White clouds at the summit still beckon me
but how dark and somber the mountain has
    become!

An evening breeze bends the water-rushes
catkin fluff flying everywhere.

Far to the east new grass greens the marshes
but here it is dusk. I go in and bar the door.

WANG WEI
(Trans. Taylor Stoehr)

Hotel

My room's shaped like a cage the sun
Puts his arm right through the window
But I who wish to smoke and dream
Use it to light my cigarette
I don't want to work I want to smoke

GUILLAUME APOLLINAIRE

(TRANS. ANNE HYDE GREET)

Summer: 6:00 A.M.

From the shadowy upstairs bedroom
of my mother-in-law's house in Hamden
I hear the neighbors' children waking.

"Ahhhhhhh," says the infant, not
unhappily. "Yes, yes, yes, yes, yes!"
replies the toddler to his mother,
who must have forbidden something.
It is hot already at this hour
and the houses are wholly open.
If she is cross with the child
anyone with ears will hear.

The slap of sprinkler water
hitting the sidewalk and street,
and the husband's deliberate footfalls
receding down the drive . . .

His Japanese sedan matches the house.
Beige, brown . . . Yesterday he washed it,
his arm thrust deep into something
that looked like a sheepskin oven mitt.

His wife had put the babies
in the shallow plastic wading
pool, and she took snapshots, trying
repeatedly to get both boys to look.
The older one's wail rose
and matched the pitch of the cicada
in a nearby tree. Why
is the sound of a spoon on a plate
next door a thing so desolate?
I think of the woman pouring a glass of juice
for the three-year-old, and watching him
spill it, knowing he *must* spill it,
seeing the ineluctable downward course
of the orange-pink liquid, the puddle
swell on the kitchen
floor beside the child's shoe.

JANE KENYON

Plainsong

A large loud raven falls from a branch
a hundred feet high, falling past
branches invisible to me,
and frozen squirrels
                    on their telephone highwires
caught in the act of taking a shortcut,
and others on the roof tops—
claws scattering across the tiles—
and smaller birds
protesting greed and bloodlust
and loud unlettered birds.
He does not stop
until he bounces down
onto the pavement in the alley
and he dances carefully, busybodily
around the brown toupee.
Or is it a squirrel
curled up in exhaustion?
The large black bird now peeks and pecks
and ponders, until I turn away and leave him
     to his work.

He hasn't learned to want
what he doesn't need or to spend
what he hasn't earned.

A white stripe under the neighbor's eave
marks the unfinished skylight
her stepfather started
until the husband found out.
One was tall and one was dark
and both men beam at the sight of a beer
and a bouncing
ball. She fell
featherlike. Her threaded
secrets delayed the world's
desire to crush her.

And in the time I took to write about the white
the band of reddish blue has disappeared,
    dropped
from above the roof
to well behind the distant silhouette
of silent houses.
The sequence in the sky is now white and gray
    and white and black.

The fat and glossy black bird has left the alley,
its brittle leaves and broken branches.
He'll have to wait another day
for springtime's florid display
of death in careless abundance.

LARRY VÉLEZ

In a Hard
Intellectual Light

In a hard intellectual light
I will kill all delight,
And I will build a citadel
Too beautiful to tell

O too austere to tell
And far too beautiful to see,
Whose evident distance
I will call the best of me.

And this light of intellect
Will shine on all my desires,
It will my flesh protect
And flare my bold constant fires,

For the hard intellectual light
Will lay the flesh with nails.
And it will keep the world bright
And closed the body's soft jails.

And from this fair edifice
I shall see, as my eyes blaze,
The moral grandeur of man
Animating all his days.

And peace will marry purpose,
And purity married to grace
Will make the human absolute
As sweet as the human face.

Until my hard vision blears,
And Poverty and Death return
In organ music like the years,
Making the spirit leap, and burn

For the hard intellectual light
That kills all delight
And brings the solemn, inward pain
Of truth into the heart again.

RICHARD EBERHART

A Room

A room does not turn its back on grief.
Anger does not excite it.
Before desire, it neither responds
nor draws back in fear.

Without changing expression,
it takes
and gives back;
not a tuft in the mattress alters.

Windowsills evenly welcome
both heat and cold.
Radiators speak or fall silent as they must.

Doors are not equivocal,
floorboards do not hesitate or startle.
Impatience does not stir the curtains,
a bed is neither irritable nor rapacious.

Whatever disquiet we sense in a room
we have brought there.

And so I instruct my ribs each morning,
pointing to hinge and plaster and wood—

    You are matter, as they are.
    See how perfectly it can be done.
    Hold, one day more, what is asked.

JANE HIRSHFIELD

The Fist

The fist clenched round my heart
loosens a little, and I gasp
brightness; but it tightens
again. When have I ever not loved
the pain of love? But this has moved

past love to mania. This has the strong
clench of the madman, this is
gripping the ledge of unreason, before
plunging howling into the abyss.

Hold hard then, heart. This way at least you live.

DEREK WALCOTT

Embrace

You know the parlor trick.
Wrap your arms around your own body
and from the back it looks like
someone is embracing you,
her hands grasping your shirt,
her fingernails teasing your neck.

From the front it is another story.
You never looked so alone,
your crossed elbows and screwy grin.
You could be waiting for a tailor
to fit you for a straitjacket,
one that would hold you really tight.

BILLY COLLINS

Mutable Earth

Are you healed or do you only think you're healed?

I told myself
from nothing
nothing could be taken away.

But can you love anyone yet?

When I feel safe, I can love.

But will you touch anyone?

I told myself
if I had nothing
the world couldn't touch me.

In the bathtub, I examine my body.
We're supposed to do that.

And your face too?
Your face in the mirror?

I was vigilant: when I touched myself
I didn't feel anything.

Were you safe then?

I was never safe, even when I was most hidden.
Even then I was waiting.

So you couldn't protect yourself?

The absolute
erodes; the boundary, the wall
around the self erodes.
If I was waiting I had been
invaded by time.

But do you think you're free?

I think I recognize the patterns of my nature.

But do you think you're free?

I had nothing
and I was still changed.
Like a costume, my numbness
was taken away. Then
hunger was added.

LOUISE GLÜCK

Reeling
WHEN YOU
GO WILD

The good news is you've sprung yourself from the prison of Hiding. No more holding yourself hostage from the world, no more waiting for some miraculous something to rescue you from misery. You're free, hungry, and determined to prove that the world has in no way kicked your ass.

You're making a comeback—great! But not so great—you're coming back with a vengeance, and it's the vengeance part that's worrisome. You're out to settle a score with the world, to show that you're as tough as any heartache the world throws at you. You're going to try everything, risk anything—being good hasn't kept you from getting hurt, so what have you got to lose by going a little wild? At least you're not sitting home letting life pass you by.

Welcome to Reeling, where you're desperate to grab on to something—anything—that will pull you into feeling alive. This is the stage where you throw yourself into the world with abandon. Blind date with the cab driver's cousin? Sure! Train for a marathon that's one week away? Why not? And while you're at it, run up your credit card at Banana Republic, join two book clubs, a gym, and a cooking class, volunteer at a shelter, plan the company retreat, scam invitations to every event in town, and try any drink or drug that comes your way.

If you're lucky in Reeling, something good will come of your manic attempts to jump-start your life—some class will reveal your vocation, or some party will introduce you to a soul mate. But we've seen Reeling friends stagger straight into pulled hamstrings, bad relationships, nasty gynecological situations, deep debt, and worse.

The initial Reeling impulse is a good one— we want to live again. No matter how much we tried to shut ourselves away in Hiding, we've been unable to resist the powerful pull of instinct, described in Virgil's "The Wave." We find ourselves joining "all the creatures on earth" in the rush to charge toward life, love, and the possibility of renewal. But as we surge forward in hope, we sometimes forget (or try to pretend we forget) that there's danger ahead—we face the possibility of crashing on the rocks or getting burned by the fire of love. We ought to temper our instinct with a little reason, a little caution—but we just can't be bothered. We're like teenagers in heat.

Which brings us conveniently to our next poem, one that perfectly illustrates this phase of adolescent hunger—the up-and-at'em penis. In "Down, Wanton, Down!" the penis (we'll just call him "Wanton," like Robert Graves) raises his "angry head" to stare down just about anything, Love or Beauty, man or beast—much to the embarrassment of his superior officer, the speaker, who tries to reason with Wanton (when shouting at him doesn't seem to work). Look, you witless Wanton, the speaker says, you're doing me no favors if you can't distinguish between man or beast! I want Beauty and Love, but they'll never swear loyalty to me if you don't learn to "think fine" and act with a little delicacy.

We're not saying you're sexually out of control in Reeling (although we know plenty of Reelers who once answered to the call of Wanton). We're saying that you're so focused on finding some release, so intent on trying everything until you hit upon happiness, that you lose the ability to choose wisely and thoughtfully. It's like grocery shopping when you're starving—you wind up with a cartful of Pringles and Ben & Jerry's.

Eventually our bad choices catch up with us, but for a while we cruise along our cocky way, convinced we've pulled a U-turn on misery. What's important is to keep moving, fill up the calendar—don't leave any time to moon over past loves or losses. Like the speaker in Andrew Marvell's "To His Coy Mistress," we can't waste precious hours on silly, idealized notions of happily ever after. We're getting older and less attractive by the second—so let's grab what we can while we can. We'd rather "tear our pleasures with rough strife"—force ourselves into feeling alive—than wait around for some fairy-tale ending we no longer believe in.

The problem is we act tougher than we really

are—we do *too* still believe in fairy-tale endings! We do *too* want to wait for happiness! This busy little life is just another form of waiting, and we know it. We don't want to keep bouncing around like this forever—we want to swoosh into some sweet spot, some home that's meant just for us. But we don't quite know how to get there, so we try on all kinds of attitudes and poses, like the speaker in Carolyn Creedon's "The Nectarine Poem." She'll become a nectarine, if that will make Tom happy, or an orange—whatever it takes, she'll change into that colorful, juicy something for Tom. Because she knows that he won't leave his wife for her the way she is now, all serious and needy—"with the silence so big it's a sound/and the wanting so big it's a weight." Tom wants a delicious something he can devour, not a feminist who tastes like rhubarb. So even though she doesn't completely want to do it, even though she hopes he cracks his tooth biting down on her, even though she knows Tom is nothing but a two-timing truffle, she tries to give him what he wants.

And this is where the bad choices *do* catch up with you—when you're so out of control with desire that you lose yourself, your reason, your core. You sacrifice your integrity, you do things you'll regret later, all because you want what you want *now*. You think if you can just grab that brass ring, whatever it is—a boyfriend, a baby, a whopping salary, a bigger home—then you'll stop spinning around on this crazy carousel of desire. Who cares if it means dumping your Birkenstocks for a Wonderbra, dating a milk-toast but marriage-minded guy, kissing up to the boss you detest— you'll do all of it, any of it, if it means you'll finally get to stop searching and wanting.

Like the waitress in Creedon's "Pub Poem," you make your "yummy heart" the "Special of the Day," available cheap to anyone who orders it. The infatuated farmer, the lonely marine, the Pub itself—the waitress will give herself to all of them, because she's desperate to feel needed and wanted. Deep down all she really wants is the love of her life, "the man who slipped away," but if she can't have him she'll take the next-best thing, or the next-to-last thing. And the more she compromises, flinging herself out in all directions, the deeper she falls into emptiness and angst.

Of course we finally fall in Reeling—we're exhausted from trying so hard to substitute activity for fulfillment, to pretend that a busy life equals a meaningful life. We've been holding our breath for what seems like "a million ebbing years," struggling to emerge in some happier life. And we're determined to keep "fighting the tide" until we get there—we refuse to crumple into Hiding again, crouching in the "back of the Pub," all tight-lipped and sour like the "dead clams and unconsummated lemons." No, we are going to get the life we want, dammit, if it kills us. And what do you know—eventually the insane pace of Reeling *does* knock us flat on our backs.

That's why we love Frank O'Hara's "Poem (Lana Turner Has Collapsed!)"—it lets us laugh at our crazy attempts to outrace unhappiness. Poor Lana Turner (va-va-voom 1950s movie star whose gangster boyfriend Johnny Stompanato was stabbed to death by Lana's teenage daughter, who claimed Johnny had raped her) has collapsed—and who wouldn't if they'd gone through everything Lana had endured! But the speaker in the poem is just as frenzied and harried as Lana must have been—until he learns that LANA TURNER HAS COLLAPSED! Not glamorous, unstoppable Lana! Heavens, no! Because if she's going down—out in picture-perfect Hollywood—he's going down, Mr. Trotting Along in the hail and snow and traffic. And we're all headed toward collapse, all of us "in such a hurry" believers.

That's where Reeling leaves us, burned out and worn down. We move from telling old Wanton the penis, "Down, boy!" to begging, "oh Lana Turner we love you get up." Our uncontrollable desire leads to our inevitable crash. Now is the time to remember—living passionately doesn't have to mean being reckless and indiscriminate. We have a brain and a soul (or a spirit, if you will), as well as emotion and instinct—we can use all of these resources to discern our purpose in the world. No, we don't want to live in the repression of Hiding or the abandon of Reeling, but yes, we do want to live committed, meaningful lives.

We're all searching for the kind of balance Elizabeth Alexander describes in "Equinox," the kind grounded in the physical laws of the universe. The word "equinox" actually refers to the time of year when the sun crosses the earth's equator, so that the length of the day is virtually equal to the length of the night. It's a perfect division of light and shadow.

The grandmother in the poem lies in an equinox of her own, poised between life and death. Like Lana Turner, she has collapsed—but unlike Lana, the grandmother does get up, if only for one last "wild/and eccentric" moment, when she rears back and slaps the nurse. We love the grandmother for that last, defiant slap at death (apologies to the nurse), for hanging on to that fierce will to live. She shows that to achieve balance between Hiding and Reeling we don't have to give up our wildness, our life force. We just have to know when to use it to good effect. We can't spend our whole lives buzzing about like dervishes, but we can't just live like dried husks either. Despite the strokes of loss or disappointment that fell us, we need to keep a vital spirit, full of venom and honey.

Being vital means acting deliberately and thoughtfully, and with a certain playfulness. Sometimes you use a little honey, sometimes you use a little venom, but always you stop to think about your choices. You're not just reacting to loss anymore; you're not just lashing out and grabbing wildly. Moving out of Reeling means growing up, trying to live according to your convictions, allowing yourself a few mistakes and a little disorder in the process. You're learning to be yourself again— not too wanton, and not "too precise in every part," just human, full of a "wild civility" (Robert Herrick, "Delight in Disorder").

You're ready to take on the hard work of slowly building who you want to be—and to realize you're not working alone. Each man in Mark Doty's "At the Gym" hoists some burden he's chosen, pushes the weight skyward in an attempt to gain some power over his flesh, "which goads with desire,/and terrifies with frailty." Each one is scared that he wants so much from life and can be hurt so badly by it. But even though the work for each man feels like his struggle alone, he can see—others have left their "salt-stain spot" on the bench, too, and others will come later.

Like the men at the gym, we're all trying collectively "to make ourselves:/something difficult/lifted, pressed or curled." And it's not just because of our vanity or because we think we deserve perfect lives—it's something more tender than that. We all want to "sweat the mark/of our presence" into the world, to be part of something bigger than ourselves. We're ready to leave the frenzy of Reeling and start shaping our purpose in the world.

The Wave

As when far off in the middle of the ocean
A breast-shaped curve of wave begins to whiten
And rise above the surface, then rolling on
Gathers and gathers until it reaches land
Huge as a mountain and crashes among the rocks
With a prodigious roar, and what was deep
Comes churning up from the bottom in mighty
    swirls
Of sunken sand and living things and water—

So in the springtime every race of people
And all the creatures on earth or in the water,
Wild animals and flocks and all the birds
In all their painted colors, all rush to charge
Into the fire that burns them: love moves them all.

VIRGIL
(Trans. Robert Pinsky)

Down, Wanton, Down!

Down, wanton, down! Have you no shame
That at the whisper of Love's name,
Or Beauty's, presto! up you raise
Your angry head and stand at gaze?

Poor bombard-captain, sworn to reach
The ravelin and effect a breach—
Indifferent what you storm or why,
So be that in the breach you die!

Love may be blind, but Love at least
Knows what is man and what mere beast;
Or Beauty wayward, but requires
More delicacy from her squires.

Tell me, my witless, whose one boast
Could be your staunchness at the post,
When were you made a man of parts
To think fine and profess the arts?

Will many-gifted Beauty come
Bowing to your bald rule of thumb,
Or Love swear loyalty to your crown?
Be gone, have done! Down, wanton, down!

ROBERT GRAVES

To His Coy Mistress

Had we but world enough, and time,
This coyness, lady, were no crime.
We would sit down, and think which way
To walk, and pass our long love's day.
Thou by the Indian Ganges' side
Shouldst rubies find: I by the tide
Of Humber would complain. I would
Love you ten years before the Flood:
And you should if you please refuse
Till the conversion of the Jews.
My vegetable love should grow
Vaster than empires, and more slow.
An hundred years should go to praise
Thine eyes, and on thy forehead gaze.
Two hundred to adore each breast:
But thirty thousand to the rest.

An age at least to every part,
And the last age should show your heart.
For, lady, you deserve this state;

Nor would I love at lower rate.
    But at my back I always hear
Time's wingéd chariot hurrying near:
And yonder all before us lie
Deserts of vast eternity.
Thy beauty shall no more be found,
Nor, in thy marble vault, shall sound
My echoing song; then worms shall try
That long preserved virginity:
And your quaint honour turn to dust;
And into ashes all my lust.
The grave's a fine and private place,
But none, I think, do there embrace.
    Now therefore, while the youthful hue
Sits on thy skin like morning dew,
And while thy willing soul transpires
At every pore with instant fires,
Now let us sport us while we may;
And now, like am'rous birds of prey,
Rather at once our time devour,

Than languish in his slow-chapped power.
Let us roll all our strength, and all
Our sweetness, up into one ball:
And tear our pleasures with rough strife
Through the iron gates of life.
Thus, though we cannot make our sun
Stand still, yet we will make him run.

ANDREW MARVELL

The Nectarine Poem

If I were a nectarine
would you be happy?
You, with your permanent press shirt
your dusty brown loafers with the pennies missing
you could bite down on me and
the juice would run down the edges of your
    moustache and
drip down
onto your heart.
Your shirt would be stained with me
as I am stained with you
my darling, my honeydew
if I were a nectarine.

If I were an orange
would you be happy?
You could peel off my skin!
You could stand in some farmer's yard

You could steal me
You could take advantage of the night to
pluck me, boldly
from some farmer's tree; I would taste the sweeter
for being forbidden fruit
as do you
my darling, my kumquat
my overripe grapefruit too long on the limb
my Tom.

If I were a button—not a fruit—
a button
missing off your precious permanent press shirt
and you found me
wedged
between the stairway and a pair of your wife's
    navy blue pumps
you could bite me
you could bite down so hard you would break
    your tooth
as I have been broken, by you
my darling, my broken toothed angel
my faulty, irregular lover
my Tom.

If I were a me,
a me,
me with big teeth and red sweater and
hair the color of thousand island dressing,
a feminist, a rhubarb,
would you be happy?
You could bite into my fuzzy neck
and the juice would run down to my sweater but
would you sit down with me
with the silence so big it's a sound
and the wanting so big it's a weight
that when I stand up
there's that rush of downward stickiness
as I want to melt, with you
my darling, my twotiming truffle
my bitter melon
my Tom.

CAROLYN CREEDON

Pub Poem

If I hold my breath for a million ebbing years,
    little oyster
waiting my tables, fighting the tide, swimming
    to hope
and still I can't open you up, love
I'll marry the fat red tomato
I got from an infatuated farmer who waits
    pleasantly
with knife and fork, to eat me.
I'll marry the warm brown York, where naked
    swimming
is like breathing, a priority, and only as dangerous
as the softshell crabs slipping away on the sandy
    floor of the river.
I'll marry my worn work shirt, stained with
    Corona and crabcake
and sweat and a little smear of cocktail sauce
    like a margin.
I'll marry each lonely marine I wait on,
he and I will picture a possible me, painting my
    toenails
bloodred in a trailer, waiting for him,

for the slippery click of the lock;
knowing it now, we look away.
I'll marry the teasing moon whose bright vowels
    dance on the water
like the Yorktown Slut, promising everything
sighing, before she slips away
what if, what if.
I'll engage my boss on his boat in thoughts of
    brastraps
and panties and other wistful trappings
which become, like breathing, a priority.
I'll marry each barnacle I scrub
bare, barely staying afloat,
while the bass slip away past the rockabye boat
    and the waves whisper
dive under, dive under, seduction is rare,
seduction is hope.
I'll marry the Pub, and slop icecold mugs of beer
onto men whose eyes seem to say that I too, am
    replaceable.
My sneakered feet will slip, I'll wed the salted
    floor that way—
slide into the sun and marry the day.
I'll marry the bent mirror in the back

where I pin up my marmalade hair
and stare at lips as red as cocktail sauce
the round everpresent planet of mouth
and fragile freckled arms who miss the man who
    slipped away.
I'll marry my beautiful brown teacher whose
    letters,
which say angst is my downfall, I read on the
    sneak
on a Budweiser box amongst the dead clams
    and unconsummated lemons
in the back of the Pub; I'll marry my downfall.
And if I fall down a hole as big as the
    Chesapeake Bay, big as my whole
yummy heart, today's Special of the Day.
I'll marry it.

CAROLYN CREEDON

Poem (Lana Turner Has Collapsed!)

Lana Turner has collapsed!
I was trotting along and suddenly
it started raining and snowing
and you said it was hailing
but hailing hits you on the head
hard so it was really snowing and
raining and I was in such a hurry
to meet you but the traffic
was acting exactly like the sky
and suddenly I see a headline
LANA TURNER HAS COLLAPSED!
there is no snow in Hollywood
there is no rain in California
I have been to lots of parties
and acted perfectly disgraceful
but I never actually collapsed
oh Lana Turner we love you get up

FRANK O'HARA

Equinox

Now is the time of year when bees are wild
and eccentric. They fly fast and in cramped
loop-de-loops, dive-bomb clusters of conversants
in the bright, late-September out-of-doors.
I have found their dried husks in my clothes.

They are dervishes because they are dying,
one last sting, a warm place to squeeze
a drop of venom or of honey.
After the stroke we thought would be her last
my grandmother came back, reared back and
    slapped

a nurse across the face. Then she stood up,
walked outside, and lay down in the snow.
Two years later there is no other way
to say, we are waiting. She is silent, light
as an empty hive, and she is breathing.

ELIZABETH ALEXANDER

Delight in Disorder

A sweet disorder in the dress
Kindles in clothes a wantonness.
A lawn about the shoulders thrown
Into a fine distractiön;
An erring lace, which here and there
Enthralls the crimson stomacher;
A cuff neglectful, and thereby
Ribbons to flow confusedly;
A winning wave, deserving note,
In the tempestuous petticoat;
A careless shoestring, in whose tie
I see a wild civility;
Do more bewitch me than when art
Is too precise in every part.

ROBERT HERRICK

At the Gym

This salt-stain spot
marks the place where men
lay down their heads,
back to the bench,

and hoist nothing
that need be lifted
but some burden they've chosen
this time: more reps,

more weight, the upward shove
of it leaving, collectively,
this sign of where we've been:
shroud-stain, negative

flashed onto the vinyl
where we push something
unyielding skyward,
gaining some power

at least over flesh,
which goads with desire,
and terrifies with frailty.
Who could say who's

added his heat to the nimbus
of our intent, here where
we make ourselves:
something difficult

lifted, pressed or curled,
Power over beauty,
power over power!
Though there's something more

tender, beneath our vanity,
our will to become objects
of desire: we sweat the mark
of our presence onto the cloth.

Here is some halo
the living made together.

MARK DOTY

Dealing

WHEN YOU
FACE FACTS

You're finally busted. There's no place left to run or hide from your Hurting, so you have to just face it head-on. It's like the climax of every action movie, where the heroes finally rip off their disguises, drop their weapons, and square off mano a mano. Only the fight you face in Dealing is with yourself, with your memories of the past and your hopes for the future. In Dealing, you're part superhero (the invincibly strong person you strive to be), part villain (the lonely, frustrated person you've become), and part ordinary Clark Kent (the real you, who just wants to live a reasonably happy life).

This battle is tougher than the one in Reeling, when you tried to wrestle the world into submission. Dealing is more about diplomacy and intelligence gathering than brute force. You're asking yourself hard questions: Why do I keep blaming everyone else for my loneliness? What truly makes me happy? What changes do I need to make on the inside before I can become the person I hope to be? You're negotiating for your own peace of mind.

Maybe you're still fixated on that perfect guy from five years ago (your soul mate—except he married your roommate), or you believe your life is forever screwed because your mother didn't love you enough, or you took a wrong turn and didn't go to law school and now you're stuck adjusting claims at State Farm. What's important is to face the reality of your life, accept, forgive, and change what you can, and then prepare to move on.

As the poets in this section tell us, it takes a great deal of self-discipline and hard work to sift the truth from the lies and figure out what's really at the center of our unhappiness. But if we want to reclaim our true selves, if we want to find our place in the world again, well then, we *deal*.

"Someone has to tidy up" after every war, Wislawa Szymborska tells us in "The End and the

Beginning." You do feel as if you've been through a war, exhausted, bloodied, and beaten down, but "someone has to shove/the rubble to the road-sides," and "someone has to trudge/through sludge and ashes," and this time that someone is you. It's not a pretty process—who wants to dig through a big horrible pile of splintered glass and bloody rags? But if you really want to move on, if you want to reach a place where you can simply lie in the grass gazing at the clouds, you've got to sort through that pile, find the treasures that are worth keeping, and sweep the rest away.

And sometimes you can't help idealizing the treasures you keep—like your memories of the past, when everything seemed more beautiful and pure than you feel now. Like the speaker in Claude McKay's "The Tropics in New York," you may long for the dewy dawns and "mystical blue skies," the old familiar ways of your childhood. You wish you had that innocence back, that ease and trust in the world. But life had its struggles then, too, if you could only remember them. And the fact is you *did* grow up (you did leave that island for New York). Just because you're older and weathered now doesn't mean you have to abandon your sense of beauty and faith in the world. You may not live on the island anymore, but the tangerines and mangoes of your child-hood past will be part of who you are forever.

Or perhaps you want to stay put in your memories of glorious, true love. You can't move forward because you think nothing will ever measure up to the perfection of what you once had. So you fixate on the fantasy of an idealized love described so beautifully in Pablo Neruda's "Night on the Island." The poem paints a picture of two lovers who are so in tune with each other that their very dreams are joined, and their kisses taste of the "depths of . . . life." But we know that the secret of life can't be found in a kiss, no matter how wild and sweet, and we know that no other person can be a cup into which we pour our gifts. Even Neruda hints that this love can't last forever—the title of the poem is "*Night* on the Island," not "*Life* on the Island."

In Dealing, you must take off the rose-colored glasses and begin to look at the past through a sharper lens of truth: Maybe you did live that passionate night or two with someone you thought you'd be connected to forever—but it didn't save you from unhappiness then, and it won't now.

So we let go of the idealized past (see it for what it was) and dig into the real past to find what's worth keeping. You know you want to keep the keen aliveness you felt when you were sixteen—which Shawn M. Durrett evokes so perfectly in "Lures." Your sensual self was wide awake—he was "all heat and skin/and smoke in throats" against a backdrop of "fall's blaze-red of sumac," and the impossible blue of the October sky. It wasn't a Pablo Neruda grand kind of romance—it was experimental, liberating, adolescent bliss. You may not have the same hormones or great body you had when you were sixteen, but you can always keep the capacity for this kind of dizzy joy.

And hold on to the memories that bring hope to the uncertain present. The speaker in Joyce Carol Oates's "Waiting on Elvis, 1956" was twenty-six, married "but still/waiting tables" and remembers when the very young (just twenty-one), still-thin Elvis swaggered into her greasy spoon like he owned the place. She's probably tired, just wants to get through her shift, but she snaps alive and flirts a little with the King, even playfully slaps at him, "feeling [her] face burn." Elvis, with his honey smile ("the kind of boy even meanness turned sweet in/his mouth"), sees that she's got plenty of edge and sass and charm left. And the waitress knows, looking back, that the world is still full of possibility, that if that could happen to her then—Elvis wanted her!—then *anything* can happen anytime, even when you're down and out.

It's a good thing that Dealing has its moments of delight like this, when you discover that even if you can't have the romanticized past back, you can always keep your heart open to beauty and hope. Because you'll need the strength of that moment to help you face the next step of Dealing—taking responsibility for some of the bad stuff in your past.

Perhaps, like the speaker in Robert Hayden's "Those Winter Sundays," you've long felt that your family didn't love or appreciate you the way you deserved. You thought your parents just filled the house with "chronic angers," so you feared them or treated them with sullen indifference when you were growing up. And you blamed them for all the relationships you've messed up in your life. But maybe, like the speaker in the poem, you can finally see not just the dramatic bad moments, but the quiet moments of effort and devotion. His father's cracked hands banked the fires that drove out the cold, and "no one ever thanked him." Now the speaker understands the "austere and lonely offices" of his father's love. Like him, maybe you can move past the lie of blame and begin to understand your own mistakes and bad choices.

If we don't reach this point in Dealing, we may wind up like the evil stepmother in Anna Swir's poem "She Does Not Remember." The subject was truly an evil stepmother, but she stubbornly refuses to remember how she made Cinderella scrub the floor and wear rags—all she knows is "that she feels cold." If she would only face up to the evil she's done, admit her mistakes, maybe even hope for forgiveness, then she might finally experience the warmth of inner peace.

Both Johnny Coley and Kim Konopka show us that dealing is not just hard work—it's a lifelong process. In "The Dogs," the speaker is convinced that he feels anger, terror, and boredom only because he has lost his lover. These feelings, he says, are like dogs that bark nonstop and "chew up everything in the apartment." If only his lover would return, the "dogs" would calm down and be good. But after his lover has left for the last time, he begins to understand that he is alone with his feelings and must learn to deal with them one by one.

For the speaker in "The Layers Between Me," facing the truth about herself and her life is a lot like housework—sometimes tedious, sometimes satisfying. She drags her dust cloth over cluttered tables and book-lined shelves, she rubs clear "the framed smiles of cherished friends," until finally she comes to a bedroom mirror, "untouched now for several seasons." She likes the way she looks in this dusty mirror, her reflection softened, lines erased—a subtle deception. But today, she is ready to face her real self, without the illusion the dust adds. Full of resolve, she wipes "the lie away"—but she knows the dust will pile up again, and in a week or a month, she'll have to face the task again. We're always going to have those specks of dust and dirt on our self-image—that's just what it means to be human.

So what's the reward for this constant cleanup? Look at the speaker in Louise Glück's "Purple Bathing Suit." She has just a few problems with the man she's chosen—for one there's that mouth. Then there's the awful purple bathing suit and the fact that no matter how many times she tells him, he *still* doesn't know how to weed; he's ostensibly working hard, but really "doing the worst job possible." In fact, if you add up all of his faults, he's "a small irritating purple thing." So why is she with him? Because she knows there is no absolutely happily-ever-after, no perfect mate— you take the good with the bad. Sure, he may be a dead loss in the garden, but at the dinner table and in bed, he's something else again. Her reward lies in the fact that she can shed her illusions and own up to her complicated feelings: in spite of all of his faults, he is *her* purple-bathing-suit man. She chooses him, she needs him, and she claims him.

Ultimately, Dealing is about facing the truth, discarding the lies and then making your own choices. By the time you're through with this internal battle, you might feel a bit like our "lingering Parents," Adam and Eve, at the end of John Milton's *Paradise Lost*. Poor old Adam and Eve have been evicted from Eden, burdened with the knowledge of good and evil—but finally conscious. Now Dealing has evicted you from your own false Paradise. You won't keep longing for an idealized past, and you aren't going to expect a miraculously perfect future. You've made peace with yourself, and you're ready to take the next step (even though it may be "wandring" and slow) toward living fully in the glorious, imperfect, *real* world.

The End and
the Beginning

After every war
someone has to tidy up.
Things won't pick
themselves up, after all.

Someone has to shove
the rubble to the roadsides
so the carts loaded with corpses
can get by.

Someone has to trudge
through sludge and ashes,
through the sofa springs,
the shards of glass,
the bloody rags.

Someone has to lug the post
to prop the wall,
someone has to glaze the window,
set the door in its frame.

No sound bites, no photo opportunities,
and it takes years.
All the cameras have gone
to other wars.

The bridges need to be rebuilt,
the railroad stations, too.
Shirtsleeves will be rolled
to shreds.

Someone, broom in hand,
still remembers how it was.
Someone else listens, nodding
his unshattered head.
But others are bound to be bustling nearby
who'll find all that
a little boring.

From time to time someone still must
dig up a rusted argument
from underneath a bush
and haul it off to the dump.

Those who knew
what this was all about
must make way for those
who know little.
And less than that.
And at last nothing less than nothing.

Someone has to lie there
in the grass that covers up
the causes and effects
with a cornstalk in his teeth,
gawking at clouds.

WISŁAWA SZYMBORSKA
(Trans. Stanisław Barańczak
and Clare Cavanagh)

The Tropics in New York

Bananas ripe and green, and ginger-root,
   Cocoa in pods and alligator pears,
And tangerines and mangoes and grape fruit,
   Fit for the highest prize at parish fairs,

Set in the window, bringing memories
   Of fruit-trees laden by low-singing rills,
And dewy dawns, and mystical blue skies
   In benediction over nun-like hills.

My eyes grew dim, and I could no more gaze;
   A wave of longing through my body swept,
And, hungry for the old, familiar ways,
   I turned aside and bowed my head and wept.

CLAUDE MCKAY

Night on the Island

All night I have slept with you
next to the sea, on the island.
Wild and sweet you were between pleasure
    and sleep,
between fire and water.

Perhaps very late
our dreams joined
at the top or at the bottom,
up above like branches moved by a common
    wind,
down below like red roots that touch.

Perhaps your dream
drifted from mine
and through the dark sea
was seeking me
as before,

when you did not yet exist,
when without sighting you
I sailed by your side,
and your eyes sought
what now—
bread, wine, love, and anger—
I heap upon you
because you are the cup
that was waiting for the gifts of my life.

I have slept with you
all night long while
the dark earth spins
with the living and the dead,
and on waking suddenly
in the midst of the shadow
my arm encircled your waist.
Neither night nor sleep
could separate us.

I have slept with you
and on waking, your mouth,
come from your dream,
gave me the taste of earth,

of sea water, of seaweed,
of the depths of your life,
and I received your kiss
moistened by the dawn
as if it came to me
from the sea that surrounds us.

PABLO NERUDA
(Trans. Donald D. Walsh)

Lures

My little sister has just turned sixteen—
her letter says she's placed an onion
under her bed, hoping to draw that perfect love.
"Honestly," she writes, *"sometimes
you don't know how lucky you are,"*

as if he was the twist of an apple's stem
in my sweaty palm, three cherries rising
to the clink of coins.

At sixteen boys *were* leaves caught
in outstretched palms, all heat and skin
and smoke in throats, as if everything
depended on fall's blaze-red of sumac,
the sky's impossible shades of October blue.

My grandmother used to say a girl
would be lucky in love if she drank
well water from a tin bucket in which three
stones were placed. I remember one day
at the lake, watching him on the other shore
in his purple t-shirt, bending
to pick up stones and throw them
out to where two men bobbed in a rowboat,
plunk of lures and voices on surface
were the muted blue tones of beach glass.

I remember thinking, *"I know exactly how
he will hold those stones,"* each cup and ease
of his hands, fingers rubbing speckled skin.
There was such knowing in those hands—
they were the push of a screen door, my body
blowing through, that tin taste in my throat
of water coming to surface, his eyes
the flat blue-gray of wet stones from the lake.

SHAWN M. DURRETT

Waiting on Elvis, 1956

This place up in Charlotte called Chuck's where I
used to waitress and who came in one night
but Elvis and some of his friends before his concert
at the Arena, I was twenty-six married but still
waiting tables and we got to joking around like you
do, and he was fingering the lace edge of my slip
where it showed below my hemline and I hadn't
    even
seen it and I slapped at him a little saying, You
sure are the one aren't you feeling my face burn
    but
he was the kind of boy even meanness turned
    sweet in
his mouth.

Smiled at me and said, Yeah honey I guess I
    sure am.

JOYCE CAROL OATES

Those Winter Sundays

Sundays too my father got up early
and put his clothes on in the blueblack cold,
then with cracked hands that ached
from labor in the weekday weather made
banked fires blaze. No one ever thanked him.

I'd wake and hear the cold splintering, breaking.
When the rooms were warm, he'd call,
and slowly I would rise and dress,
fearing the chronic angers of that house,

Speaking indifferently to him,
who had driven out the cold
and polished my good shoes as well.
What did I know, what did I know
of love's austere and lonely offices?

ROBERT HAYDEN

She Does Not Remember

She was an evil stepmother.
In her old age she is slowly dying
in an empty hovel.

She shudders
like a clutch of burnt paper.
She does not remember that she was evil.
But she knows
that she feels cold.

ANNA SWIR
(Trans. Czeslaw Milosz
and Leonard Nathan)

The Dogs

After you and I were separated
My terror came back. My irritation
And my anger and my boredom—
All of them connected, I thought,
To you—were still there.
Like dogs I was keeping for you
Anytime anyone approached
They thought it was you
And either got away from me or tried to.
So when we were reunited
I thought well finally someone else
Can look after these dogs. You said,
You like your dogs better than you do me,
Looking through your address book
For someone to call. I said,
They're always so good when you're here.
You have no idea
What it's like trying to walk them
And they chew up everything in the apartment.
They're your dogs. You said,
They're not my dogs. I hate dogs.
You ought to put them in the car,

Drive them way out in the country somewhere,
And leave them,
If you don't enjoy them.
They were barking and fighting,
Knocking things over,
Not ten minutes after we separated again,
For the last time.
Boy this is great I thought.
And if I get bored with them
There's always my terror.

JOHNNY COLEY

The Layers Between Me

My dust knows I will come for it
to glide my dampened cloth over
cluttered table, straight back chairs
and book lined shelves.
Careful not to persuade a wind
I linger through each room,
wiping new the summer souvenirs
of distant lands and rubbing clear
the framed smiles of cherished friends.

With twisted and tired rag I finish
my way toward a bedroom mirror,
which waits more patiently,
untouched now for several seasons.
Here the many layers have
softened my reflection and
I have grown fond of this
subtle deception.

But today I pause to run
my finger through the days.
I trace my oval face, circle eyes,
smudge line for narrow lips
then draw a halo
above my head and smile.
Slowly,
I wipe the lie away
to let my dust begin again.

KIM KONOPKA

Purple Bathing Suit

I like watching you garden
with your back to me in your purple bathing suit:
your back is my favorite part of you,
the part furthest away from your mouth.

You might give some thought to that mouth.
Also to the way you weed, breaking
the grass off at ground level
when you should pull it up by the roots.

How many times do I have to tell you
how the grass spreads, your little
pile notwithstanding, in a dark mass which
by smoothing over the surface you have finally
fully obscured? Watching you

stare into space in the tidy
rows of the vegetable garden, ostensibly
working hard while actually
doing the worst job possible, I think

you are a small irritating purple thing
and I would like to see you walk off the face of
    the earth
because you are all that's wrong with my life
and I need you and I claim you.

LOUISE GLÜCK

Excerpt from
Paradise Lost

In either hand the hastning Angel caught
Our lingring Parents, and to th' Eastern Gate
Led them direct, and down the Cliff as fast
To the subjected Plaine; then disappeer'd.
They looking back, all th' Eastern side beheld
Of Paradise, so late thir happie seat,
Wav'd over by that flaming Brand, the Gate
With dreadful Faces throng'd and fierie Armes:
Som natural tears they drop'd, but wip'd them
    soon;
The World was all before them, where to choose
Thir place of rest, and Providence thir guide:
They hand in hand with wandring steps and slow,
Through *Eden* took thir solitarie way.

JOHN MILTON

Healing

WHEN YOU
FIND YOURSELF

Hallelujah, you're headed for Healing. You are done with being eaten alive by anger and bitterness (Hurting), shutting yourself off from both joy and sorrow (Hiding), acting wildly on every self-destructive impulse (Reeling), and facing up to your unhappiness (Dealing). You've earned your shot at a little joy, a chance to try your newfound confidence and hope. And so you are ready to begin again, to rediscover your true self and your true direction.

This time around, you know you aren't setting yourself up for disappointment. You understand that, for all its pleasures, the world is imperfect— friends may leave, lovers will sometimes betray you, and, well, you're a little imperfect yourself. You may forever be ten pounds overweight, and sometimes you are too swamped at work or too tired to be the ideal friend yourself. But you are determined to be as loving and faithful a friend as is possible, to do work in the world that matters, and to respect and love yourself—because that's where it all begins.

So the poems in this section are about new beginnings. "After a long wet season the rain's let up," says Marie Ponsot in "Better." Yes, things are not absolutely fabulous, you haven't found the man or job of your dreams, but in a small, measured way, things are better. It may not be a perfect day, but at least it's not raining and you have found "a figured stillness where no nightmares slide." You are ready to breach the world's barriers on your own terms, to "come, eyes wide, outside."

If you're not quite ready to sing a song of absolute joy, if you need a quick jump start back into the world, well then, says the speaker in Linda Pastan's "Petit Dejeuner," you can "trick" yourself back into the rush of life. This time it's no sad parlor trick; in fact, it's more like a magician's delicious sleight of hand. The wily French do it every day—they reel themselves up into morning with a crisp, buttery croissant, a sweet little mouthful of air and light. Neither starving nor stuffing yourself, you are now wise enough to know how to savor life. So you bite into the just-right croissant and welcome once again the "sweet ceremony" of the world. Great trick, we say, and a good beginning.

And you might want to stop and hold here for a moment while you contemplate your first tentative move—to relish your very own "morning of buttered toast/of coffee, sweetened, with milk," to notice the flurry of chickadees. In "Not-Yet," Jane Hirshfield reminds us of the risks that come with venturing back into the world. Even though we have "turned [our] blessings" into the light and are grateful for what we have, we are also fully aware that the world can rip us apart again, that we can become lost, dead, shattered, fractured, and silenced. So we might want to hang back with the "single cardinal" on the empty branch for just another instant of "not-yet-now" before we launch fully into Healing.

But claiming our place in the world again doesn't have to be so scary, especially if we start by perfecting the art of the kiss-off. Instead of worrying about what we're afraid of losing, we can focus instead on what we no longer need. We did that hard internal work in Dealing, figuring out what to keep and what to leave behind. Now it's time to put it all into action. So it's goodbye to insecurity; so long, pretense; see ya to everything and everyone keeping you from being who you are. You're not angry about the past any longer, just eager to start fresh. When you free yourself like this, you find yourself—that's the beauty of the kind and careful kiss-off.

We think Galway Kinnell's "The Correspondence School Instructor Says Goodbye to His Poetry Students" is the perfect example of a loving kiss-off. He's had it, this poor teacher—with his students, the Miami Beach urologist, the West Coast brassiere manufacturer, and the San Quentin Nazi, and their terrible poems. But he doesn't *hate* them—in fact, he did care, he did read every poem, and most important, he *did* say what he thought was the truth. But they were smothering him, and in the end, he feels only pity, which is no basis for a relationship. He *must* say goodbye because he is finally ready to write his own poems, to live his own life.

What's surprising is how little you will miss the things you'll kiss off in Healing—and how much you'll appreciate what you find in yourself. The speaker in Langston Hughes's "Homecoming" loses his girlfriend but finds he's left with a *whole* lot of room—and that's not such a bad thing because it means that *he* is still whole. He can stretch out on that bed and figure out what he's going to do with that all room, and how he'll make it his own again.

This is where finding yourself becomes fun. You're discovering what you're capable of. You're lightened and lifted, no longer burdened by self-pity, anger, or grief. Anyone can scream "fuck off!" the way you did back in Hurting, but it takes patience and craft to achieve a sweet but firm kiss-off. And the more you practice saying goodbye to unrealistic expectations and conventions, the better you feel about yourself. You stop cursing the couples who don't invite single you to their dinner parties and throw your own party instead. You stop making fun of your idiot boss and start looking for more meaningful work. You dump the grapefruit diet, the wrinkle cure, the friends who only call you when their significant others are busy, and the low-rise jeans you can't wear sitting down.

In Healing we joyfully begin the real business of fulfilling our purpose and promise. What was fake and plastic in us becomes real and powerful—like the doll turned naval officer in Lyn Lifshin's "Navy Barbie." Barbie has traded in her cameo choker, grating garters, and high-heeled platform shoes for a crisp white uniform and natural hair. She's joined the Navy! She reads! She smiles because she reads! And for the first time, Barbie is authentic, her true self. Who would have guessed—the real Barbie ranks.

If Barbie can do it, we can do it—discover who we really are and earn our right to rank. If we reject the stereotype of who we're supposed to be—the workaholic, the desperate single woman, the good daughter—we learn to become who we want to be. The more we exert our independence, the more we develop our individuality. And even if others continue to expect only the stereotype, even if they get angry at us for changing, we will stay true to ourselves, like the speaker in Lucille Clifton's "why some people be mad at me sometimes." We are finally able to face the world on our terms, and we're proud of our new strength.

In Healing, we're ourselves again, only ten times better (like the Grinch after his heart grew). We finally give ourselves over to our real passions, lose ourselves in the purity of our desires, savor the moments where every point in the universe converges to create a sweet spot of perfection (not a perfect life—there is no such thing—but a perfect *moment*). In Wallace Stevens's "The House Was Quiet and the World Was Calm," the simple act of reading a book becomes "perfection of thought." You know how it is when you can't put down a book, when the room and its noise disappear and the characters come alive in your head. This is what you experience once you've truly found yourself. You become like the reader in the quiet house on the perfect summer night—calm and absorbed, leaning into the truth of the moment.

Or you become the happy loner in William Carlos Williams's "Danse Russe," who celebrates being not a husband, not a father, but just himself, in all his gleeful, grotesque nakedness. Who hasn't pranced before the mirror or sung badly in the shower when no one else is around? When you're comfortable with who you are, self-consciousness falls away, and you're free to enjoy your own glorious independence. Who wouldn't dance around in joy when they discover that being alone doesn't have to mean being lonely?

String a few of these moments together and the next thing you know, you are (gasp!) HAPPY. In Jane Kenyon's poem "The Suitor," the speaker is simply lying in bed when she notices the tree outside the window and how the leaves turn all at once "like a school of fish." In this light, shimmery moment, she suddenly understands that she is happy, that for months this feeling has been coming closer and closer—like a timid suitor. And even though we know in Healing that loss and pain and grief will surely call again, we have discovered how to recognize and hold on to these moments of joy.

The final step of Healing becomes easy. We are no longer just better. We don't have to trick ourselves into feeling alive. Of course croissants are delicious, but an occasional oatmeal morning is just fine. Our eyes are wide open and our wounds are barely scars. We have found our true strength, and we're excited to be in the world.

Better

After a long wet season the rain's let up.
The list my life was on was critical;
reproach soaked it and infected my ears.
I hid, deaf and blind, my skin my hospital,
in the inoperable ache of fear.

Today the rain stops. I can hear! Trees drip.
They spatter & whisper as I walk their
breathing avenue. The wind has died back;
edge-catching light elaborates the air.

From the road car-tunes rush close then slacken.
I climb the green hill. There at last I reach
a figured stillness where no nightmares slide.

Green leaves turn inside out to grow. They breach
their barriers. I come, eyes wide, outside.

MARIE PONSOT

Petit Dejeuner

I sing a song
of the croissant
and of the wily French
who trick themselves daily
back to the world
for its sweet ceremony.
Ah to be reeled
up into morning
on that crisp,
buttery
hook.

LINDA PASTAN

Not-Yet

Morning of buttered toast;
of coffee, sweetened, with milk.

Out the window,
snow-spruces step from their cobwebs.
Flurry of chickadees, feeding then gone.
A single cardinal stipples an empty branch—
one maple leaf lifted back.

I turn my blessings like photographs into the
    light;
over my shoulder the god of Not-Yet looks on:

Not-yet-dead, not-yet-lost, not-yet-taken.
Not-yet-shattered, not-yet-sectioned,
not-yet-strewn.

Ample litany, sparing nothing I hate or love,
not-yet-silenced, not-yet-fractured, not-yet-.

Not-yet-not.

I move my ear a little closer to that humming
    figure,
I ask him only to stay.

JANE HIRSHFIELD

The Correspondence School Instructor Says Goodbye to His Poetry Students

Goodbye, lady in Bangor, who sent me
snapshots of yourself, after definitely hinting
you were beautiful; goodbye,
Miami Beach urologist, who enclosed plain
brown envelopes for the return of your *very*
"Clinical Sonnets"; goodbye, manufacturer
of brassieres on the Coast, whose eclogues
give the fullest treatment in literature yet
to the sagging breast motif; goodbye, you in
    San Quentin,
who wrote, "Being German my hero is Hitler,"
instead of "Sincerely yours," at the end of long,
neat-scripted letters demolishing
the pre-Raphaelites:

I swear to you, it was just my way
of cheering myself up, as I licked
the stamped, self-addressed envelopes,
the game I had

of trying to guess which one of you, this time,
had poisoned his glue. I did care.
I did read each poem entire.
I did say what I thought was the truth
in the mildest words I knew. And now,
in this poem, or chopped prose, not any better,
I realize, than those troubled lines
I kept sending back to you,
I have to say I am relieved it is over:
at the end I could feel only pity
for that urge toward more life
your poems kept smothering in words, the smell
of which, days later, would tingle
in your nostrils as new, God-given impulses
to write.

Goodbye,
you who are, for me, the postmarks again
of shattered towns—Xenia, Burnt Cabins,
    Hornell—
their loneliness
given away in poems, only their solitude kept.

GALWAY KINNELL

Homecoming

I went back in the alley
And I opened up my door.
All her clothes was gone:
She wasn't home no more.

I pulled back the covers,
I made down the bed.
A *whole* lot of room
Was the only thing I had.

LANGSTON HUGHES

Navy Barbie

wants to see the world,
she does get a little
seasick but likes
the white uniform, tho
the skirt is a little
too loose and long for
her taste. Still it might
be a change she can go
with. Actually the sequins
dug into her shoulders,
the ballerina tulle
scratched, and tho it was
kept secret, fun fur
made her sneeze. And
forget the Parisian
Bonjour look: that was
the worst, a cameo
choker size of a plum
or a small coconut
wedged against her larynx,
so she says when I try
to say yes or no it

scraped, and the lace
under my arms—talk
about sandpaper. But
the worst was those fish
net hose, rough, and the
garter, Jesus, grating,
my toes burned from that
pattern, crammed into
high-heeled platform
open-toes and the hair
piece with feathers. At
least in the navy they've
actually, she smiles,
given me something to
read. My hair is natural.
I'm authentic. First
Class Petty Officer.
I finally am more than
just a pretty: I rank

LYN LIFSHIN

why some people be mad at me sometimes

they ask me to remember
but they want me to remember
their memories
and i keep on remembering
mine.

LUCILLE CLIFTON

The House Was Quiet and the World Was Calm

The house was quiet and the world was calm.
The reader became the book; and summer night

Was like the conscious being of the book.
The house was quiet and the world was calm.

The words were spoken as if there was no book,
Except that the reader leaned above the page,

Wanted to lean, wanted much most to be
The scholar to whom his book is true, to whom

The summer night is like a perfection of thought.
The house was quiet because it had to be.

The quiet was part of the meaning, part of the
    mind:
The access of perfection to the page.

And the world was calm. The truth in a calm world
In which there is no other meaning, itself

Is calm, itself is summer and night, itself
Is the reader leaning late and reading there.

WALLACE STEVENS

Danse Russe

If when my wife is sleeping
and the baby and Kathleen
are sleeping
and the sun is a flame-white disc
in silken mists
above shining trees,—
if I in my north room
dance naked, grotesquely
before my mirror
waving my shirt round my head
and singing softly to myself:
"I am lonely, lonely.
I was born to be lonely,
I am best so!"
If I admire my arms, my face,
my shoulders, flanks, buttocks
against the yellow drawn shades,—

Who shall say I am not
the happy genius of my household?

WILLIAM CARLOS WILLIAMS

The Suitor

We lie back to back. Curtains
lift and fall,
like the chest of someone sleeping.
Wind moves the leaves of the box elder;
they show their light undersides,
turning all at once
like a school of fish.
Suddenly I understand that I am happy.
For months this feeling
has been coming closer, stopping
for short visits, like a timid suitor.

JANE KENYON

Chai 1924–2000

for Yehuda Amichai

Page of sand, scab-flakes of ink;

page of sand, page of skin:
where are you now?

On the tongue, life is a verb
and death, a proverb:
Apple eats apple-blossom,

seed eats the apple. . . .
Your name, in the macaroni
of tongues, Ah-me-*hide*,
foriegn and sentimental

as the pendant *Chai*—life—
noosing the ancients of St. Pete
waiting for the Early Bird Special

—or the girls in Bolinas
you saw loosening

their tefillin-strap

bikinis: souls
opening and closing,

a prayer drifting everywhere
but up—
Proverbial waves lap

a beach of crumbs.
Letters swirl in fat broth,
a name is lifted to the lips;
waiters wipe

the clock face clean.
Drop the page,
come out. *Come out:*

the body is an apple
to the seed,

the body is a seed in the earth.

DAVID GEWANTER

Believing

WHEN YOU
STAY STRONG

Here's the scary thing about reaching Believing. No doubt about it—you're really happy. You're grounded in good relationships and meaningful work, amazed and grateful that somehow this is your life. But the better things get, the more you find yourself waiting for the sky to cave in again. You're thrilled with the too-good-to-be-trueness of every day, and terrified that you'll screw it all up somehow. It's as if you just won the Super Bowl and you're headed to Disneyworld, but all you can think about is getting thrown from a roller coaster or having to watch Bambi's mother get blown away by the hunters again.

No, you haven't landed in some Happiness theme park. You're still in the same world that once crushed your spirit and left you forsaken. But the great thing is *you're* different now. Sure the world can still slam you around, but you've worked hard to build hope and courage. You have a center, and it's going to hold.

Still, you may get a little scared or nervous sometimes, and you may need reminders of how and why you built that core. So we filled this section with exhilarating, comforting poems aimed at helping you keep the faith in yourself and the world.

Take a look at "Sadie's Poem," for starters. This is how our four-year-old friend Sadie approaches the world—with absolute confidence and joy. She's not quite sure what the day holds for her—will it be eenie, meenie, minie, or moe? But it doesn't really matter because there's this hot-diggitty fire in her toe! She's itching to move, to run, to explore. And wherever her choices take her, she's going to grab her butt and not let go—she's going to hang on to herself and jump into the day.

"Sadie's Poem" cracks us up, but it also calls us to take the same approach to life, to trust that fire in the toe. The key, we think, is to free yourself from conventional standards of happiness. Stop thinking you have to keep up with everyone else, want what they want, acquire what they acquire (the husband, the baby, the summer home, the SUV). There is no one "right" way to be happy—you get to pick your own way, you get to follow your own fire. Sadie already knows this— she took a conventional nursery rhyme, dumped the parts she didn't like, and created something entirely new, in a voice she owns and respects. She followed her own butt-grabbing philosophy and created a poem that is unmistakably, uniquely Sadie.

We think you can do the same thing with your life. Stop sweating the big choices that make you fear the future and pull a Sadie instead. Remember that whatever you choose, minie or moe, you'll be okay if you just trust your own sensibilities. And be sure to pay attention to the tiny things around you that burn with intensity (that fire in the toe)— that's where you'll find the beauty and inspiration you need to keep believing in yourself.

So instead of walking past the poor old woman munching on a plum in William Carlos Williams's "To a Poor Old Woman," stop and really look at her. You could see just an old paper bag woman slurping fruit in the street and think, "How pathetic." Or you could drop your uptight judgments, open your eyes, and glimpse a moment of pure pleasure and comfort, a moment as perfect as a ripe plum. And you'd carry that delicious moment of solace with you the rest of the day.

That's the only way to live in Believing—stay open to moments of revelation and grace, even in the most unlikely places. The speaker in Elizabeth Bishop's "Filling Station," for example, finds herself in a filthy gas station, run by an oil-soaked, monkey-suited father and his greasy sons. Yuck, ick, disgusting, is all she can think at first. But then she notices the garish comic books, the big dim doily, the hairy begonia—and even though she wants to dismiss it all as horribly tacky, she instead finds herself deeply moved by these little signs of home, these proud attempts at beauty. "Somebody embroidered the doily," and "somebody waters the plant." Maybe "somebody loves us all," she thinks. Even her, a high-strung automobile of a yuppie, even this imperfect filling station we call the world.

What a relief to experience moments like these

in Believing, when you know with certainty that you're part of something grander than yourself. Call it an epiphany, or like poet James Wright, call it "A Blessing," to find yourself rooted in a place of such hope and tenderness that you feel "that if I stepped out of my body I would break/into blossom." You have access to this kind of serene beauty because you've made the effort to find these moments, to "step over the barbed wire into the pasture" where the Indian ponies wait with eyes full of kindness.

Of course these simple little epiphanies are harder to come by when ordinary chaos is erupting around you—deadlines and family crises and flat tires. Sometimes everything seems so complicated and crazy that even though you know you're Believing and all, yadda, yadda, yadda, you just can't figure out how to keep everything together.

That's when Gerard Manley Hopkins might tell you to pull another Sadie—turn convention on its head. Instead of cursing the world, take a minute to thank your lucky stars that you're part of a place this complex, this rich, this full of dappled beauty. Of course things get complicated—the world offers us everything: "All things counter, original, spare, strange." We need the slow in order to appreciate the swift, the sweet to complement the sour, the dim to give full glory to everything adazzle. Sometimes this spotted, couple-colored world might overwhelm us, but we've got to put it in perspective. We all have a place in the abiding order and the beauty that "is past change" of our intricate universe.

While we're praising the pied beauty of the world, we may want to take a shot at appreciating and accepting our own contradictory selves. All of us are a jumble of impulse and restraint, emotion and reason, the sacred and the profane—and that includes the Pope himself, Sharon Olds suggests in "The Pope's Penis." At our best we are bells waiting to ring in praise of goodness, we are striving toward the divine, but most of the time our halos are strictly human. What more could we hope for in an imperfect world?

Even our mixed-up families—so irritating! so burdensome!—can shine with a dappled charm, once we free ourselves to really see them. The speaker in Gregory Djanikian's "Immigrant Picnic" tries hard to be the stereotypical all-

American guy, with his hot dogs on the grill and his "hat shaped/like the state of Pennsylvania." His family drives him nuts with their misunderstandings of English idioms and their irrepressible bad jokes. But once the speaker throws up his hands and stops trying to force them into some sitcom picture of an American family (and he's thinking Brady Bunch, not Costanzas), he's free to see them for who they are: the jumbled-up people who love him.

So instead of wishing things were simpler (like a boring old nursery rhyme anyone could recite), sometimes we need to celebrate everything that's mixed up ("Sadie's Poem"!). That's the fun of vacations like the one described in Lynne McMahon's "We Take Our Children to Ireland"—we get away from the usual routine, kiss off comfort, and fall into adventures that change the way we see everything. Like the kids—and the parents—in McMahon's poem. At first they're stopped cold by the cheerful profanity they hear in Ireland. But soon a "fuck off, will ye" doesn't even faze them—they know it's meant lovingly, teasingly. And they become converts, offering their own "grand responses to everyday events" in Belfast. So your breakfast isn't just good, it's brilliant. Your crust is gorgeous. Even the "shite" smeared on the face of two-year-old Jack is brilliant and gorgeous.

This is the kind of happiness you want in Believing—not the kind you can shield from the elements, like some Martha Stewart garden, but a brilliant assemblage of "grand responses to everyday events," rooted in love, humor, and glorious shite, thriving in full view of the barbed wire and turf fires.

Believing in yourself isn't about finding a perfect plateau and staying there. It's about being secure enough to see change as an opportunity for growth, no matter how much you like things the way they are. Look at "Emily Dickinson and Elvis Presley in Heaven." Emily doesn't rest on her laurels as the Belle of Amherst, and Elvis doesn't strut around being King. Who needs a heaven where you spend all day being the same old thing you used to be, anyway? No, these two shake it up, try new things, challenge and delight each other. They'd rather rock the house where "God wears blue suede shoes," then dawdle on some quiet cloud for eternity.

In "Sister Lou," Sterling A. Brown tells us that maybe we can have that kind of rocking heaven right here on earth. Maybe we can approach every day the way Sister Lou approaches Paradise. After a lifetime of Jim Crow indignities, Sister Lou finally reaches heaven, but she doesn't expect fancy harps and angels. Instead she finds joy in earthly pleasures, like teaching Martha how to make greengrape jellies or giving Lazarus a passel of her Golden Biscuits. Heaven is a neighborhood where people know and care for one another, where you can visit with Jesus for a spell and joke awhile with Jonah. If we can learn to live that way here and now—to forgive all the betrayals we've endured, the way Sister Lou rubs the poor head of mixed-up Judas; to face the world with courage and kindness, the way Sister Lou always follows the rules of her raising—then maybe every day we'll find ourselves in a life with windows "openin' on cherry trees an' plum trees/Bloomin' everlastin'."

In Believing, you're finally free to live in your

own unconventional heaven on earth. You're not looking for uninterrupted bliss, you just want to be able to maintain trust in yourself and the world. You want to know that whatever comes, you'll face it with bedrock integrity, grace, and acceptance.

The speaker in Grace Paley's "Here" epitomizes the way we want to feel in the ultimate stage of *Kiss Off*—simply free to be who we are. Somehow this laughing "old woman with heavy breasts/and a nicely mapped face" makes us think of Sadie. It's that butt-grabbing, fire-in-the-toe sensibility that we love in them both. This grandmother isn't afraid to age, to sit with her "stout thighs apart under/a big skirt," to enjoy the sweat of the summertime—she is utterly content to be here in her garden, still full of desire to kiss the "sweet explaining lips" of her old man.

This is what we hope for all of us who have been through the pain of loss—that one day we'll be able to look at our lives with the contentment of the grandmother in her garden, that we'll be able to ask ourselves, "How did this happen?" and answer, "Well that's who I wanted to be."

Sadie's Poem

Eenie, meenie, minie, moe,
There's a fire in my toe.
Grab your butt and don't let go!

SADIE LISK HIGHSMITH

To a Poor Old Woman

munching a plum on
the street a paper bag
of them in her hand

They taste good to her
They taste good
to her. They taste
good to her

You can see it by
the way she gives herself
to the one half
sucked out in her hand

Comforted
a solace of ripe plums
seeming to fill the air
They taste good to her

WILLIAM CARLOS WILLIAMS

Filling Station

Oh, but it is dirty!
—this little filling station,
oil-soaked, oil-permeated
to a disturbing, over-all
black translucency.
Be careful with that match!

Father wears a dirty,
oil-soaked monkey suit
that cuts him under the arms,
and several quick and saucy
and greasy sons assist him
(it's a family filling station),
all quite thoroughly dirty.

Do they live in the station?
It has a cement porch
behind the pumps, and on it
a set of crushed and grease-
impregnated wickerwork;
on the wicker sofa
a dirty dog, quite comfy.

Some comic books provide
the only note of color—
of certain color. They lie
upon a big dim doily
draping a taboret
(part of the set), beside
a big hirsute begonia.

Why the extraneous plant?
Why the taboret?
Why, oh why, the doily?
(Embroidered in daisy stitch
with marguerites, I think,
and heavy with gray crochet.)

Somebody embroidered the doily.
Somebody waters the plant,
or oils it, maybe. Somebody
arranges the rows of cans
so that they softly say:
ESSO—SO—SO—SO
to high-strung automobiles.
Somebody loves us all.

ELIZABETH BISHOP

A Blessing

Just off the highway to Rochester, Minnesota,
Twilight bounds softly forth on the grass.
And the eyes of those two Indian ponies
Darken with kindness.
They have come gladly out of the willows
To welcome my friend and me.
We step over the barbed wire into the pasture
Where they have been grazing all day, alone.
They ripple tensely, they can hardly contain
    their happiness
That we have come.
They bow shyly as wet swans. They love each
    other.
There is no loneliness like theirs.
At home once more,
They begin munching the young tufts of spring
    in the darkness.
I would like to hold the slenderer one in my arms,
For she has walked over to me
And nuzzled my left hand.

She is black and white,
Her mane falls wild on her forehead,
And the light breeze moves me to caress her
    long ear
That is delicate as the skin over a girl's wrist.
Suddenly I realize
That if I stepped out of my body I would break
Into blossom.

JAMES WRIGHT

Pied Beauty

Glory be to God for dappled things—
    For skies of couple-colour as a brinded cow;
        For rose-moles all in stipple upon trout that
           swim;
Fresh-firecoal chestnut-falls; finches' wings;
    Landscape plotted and pieced—fold, fallow,
        and plough;
        And áll trádes, their gear and tackle and trim.

All things counter, original, spare, strange;
    Whatever is fickle, freckled (who knows how?)
        With swift, slow; sweet, sour; adazzle, dim;
He fathers-forth whose beauty is past change:
           Praise him.

GERARD MANLEY HOPKINS

The Pope's Penis

It hangs deep in his
robes, a delicate clapper at the center of a bell.
It moves when he moves, a ghostly fish
in a halo of silver seaweed, the hair swaying in
  the dark and the heat—and at night,
while his eyes sleep, it stands up in praise of God.

SHARON OLDS

Immigrant Picnic

It's the Fourth of July, the flags
are painting the town,
the plastic forks and knives
are laid out like a parade.

And I'm grilling, I've got my apron,
I've got potato salad, macaroni, relish,
I've got a hat shaped
like the state of Pennsylvania.

I ask my father what's his pleasure
and he says, "Hot dog, medium rare,"
and then, "Hamburger, sure,
what's the big difference,"
as if he's really asking.

I put on hamburgers *and* hot dogs,
slice up the sour pickles and Bermudas,
uncap the condiments. The paper napkins
are fluttering away like lost messages.

"You're running around," my mother says,
"like a chicken with its head loose."

"Ma," I say, "you mean *cut off*,
loose and *cut off* being as far apart
as, say, *son* and *daughter*."

She gives me a quizzical look as though
I've been caught in some impropriety.
"I love you and your sister just the same," she says.
"Sure," my grandmother pipes in,
"you're both our children, so why worry?"

That's not the point I begin telling them,
and I'm comparing words to fish now,
like the ones in the sea at Port Said,
or like birds among the date palms by the Nile,
unrepentantly elusive, wild.

"Sonia," my father says to my mother,
"what the hell is he talking about?"
"He's on a ball," my mother says.

"That's *roll!*" I say, throwing up my hands,
"as in hot dog, hamburger, dinner roll. . . ."

"And what about *roll out the barrels?*" my mother
    asks,
and my father claps his hands, "Why sure," he
    says,
"let's have some fun," and launches
into a polka, twirling my mother
around and around like the happiest top,

and my uncle is shaking his head, saying
"You could grow nuts listening to us,"

and I'm thinking of pistachios in the Sinai
burgeoning without end,
pecans in the South, the jumbled
flavor of them suddenly in my mouth,
wordless, confusing,
crowding out everything else.

GREGORY DJANIKIAN

We Take Our Children to Ireland

What will they remember best? The barbed wire
still looped around the Belfast airport,
the building-high Ulster murals—
but those were fleeting, car window sights,
more likely the turf fires lit each night,
the cups of tea their father brought
and the buttered soda farls, the sea wall
where they leaped shrieking into the Irish Sea
and emerged, purpling, to applause;
perhaps the green castle at Carrickfergus,
but more likely the candy store
with its alien crisps—vinegar? they ask,
prawn cocktail? Worcestershire leek?
More certainly still the sleekly syllabled
odd new words, gleet and shite,
and grand responses to everyday events:
How was your breakfast? Brilliant.
How's your crust? Gorgeous.
Everything after that was gorgeous,
brilliant. How's your gleeted shite?
And the polite indictment from parents
everywhere, the nicely dressed matrons

pushing prams, brushing away their older kids
with a Fuck off, will ye? Which stopped
our children cold. Is the water cold,
they asked Damian, before they dared it.
No, he said, it's not cold, it's
fooking cold, ye idjits.
And the mundane hyperbole of rebuke—
you little puke, I'll tear your arm off
and beat you with it, I'll row you out to sea
and drop you, I'll bury you in sand
and top you off with rocks—
to which the toddler would contentedly nod
and continue to drill his shovel
into the sill. All this will play on
long past the fisherman's cottage and farmer's
slurry, the tall hedgerows lining the narrow
drive up the coast, the most beautiful
of Irish landscapes indelibly fixed
in the smeared face of two-year-old Jack—
Would you look at that, his father said
to Ben and Zach, shite everywhere, brilliant.
Gorgeous, they replied. And meant it.

LYNNE MCMAHON

Emily Dickinson and
Elvis Presley in Heaven

They call each other E. Elvis picks
wildflowers near the river and brings
them to Emily. She explains half-rhymes to him.

In heaven Emily wears her hair long, sports
Levis and western blouses with rhinestones.
Elvis is lean again, wears baggy trousers

and T-shirts, a letterman's jacket from Tupelo
     High.
They take long walks and often hold hands.
She prefers they remain just friends. Forever.

Emily's poems now contain naugahyde, Cadillacs,
Electricity, jets, TV, Little Richard and Richard
Nixon. The rock-a-billy rhythm makes her smile.

Elvis likes himself with style. This afternoon
he will play guitar and sing "I Taste a Liquor
Never Brewed" to the tune of "Love Me Tender."

Emily will clap and harmonize. Alone
in their cabins later, they'll listen to the river
and nap. They will not think of Amherst

or Las Vegas. They know why God made them
roommates. It's because America
was their hometown. It's because

God is a thing
without feathers. It's because
God wears blue suede shoes.

HANS OSTROM

Sister Lou

Honey
When de man
Calls out de las' train
You're gonna ride,
Tell him howdy.

Gather up yo' basket
An' yo' knittin' an' yo' things,
An' go on up an' visit
Wid frien' Jesus fo' a spell.

Show Marfa
How to make yo' greengrape jellies,
An' give po' Lazarus
A passel of them Golden Biscuits.

Scald some meal
Fo' some rightdown good spoonbread
Fo' li'l box-plunkin' David.

An' sit aroun'
An' tell them Hebrew Chillen
All yo' stories. . . .

Honey
Don't be feared of them pearly gates,
Don't go 'round to de back,
No mo' dataway
Not evah no mo'.

Let Michael tote yo' burden
An' yo' pocketbook an' evah thing
'Cept yo' Bible,
While Gabriel blows somp'n
Solemn but loudsome
On dat horn of his'n.

Honey
Go Straight on to de Big House,
An' speak to yo' God
Widout no fear an' tremblin'.

Then sit down
An' pass de time of day awhile.

Give a good talkin' to
To yo' favorite 'postle Peter,
An' rub the po' head
Of mixed-up Judas,
An' joke awhile wid Jonah.

Then, when you gits de chance,
Always rememberin' yo' raisin',
Let 'em know youse tired
Jest a mite tired.

Jesus will find yo' bed fo' you
Won't no servant evah bother wid yo' room.
Jesus will lead you
To a room wid windows
Openin' on cherry trees an' plum trees
Bloomin' everlastin'.

An' dat will be yours
Fo' keeps.

Den take yo' time. . . .
Honey, take yo' blessed time.

STERLING A. BROWN

Here

Here I am in the garden laughing
an old woman with heavy breasts
and a nicely mapped face

how did this happen
well that's who I wanted to be

at last   a woman
in the old style   sitting
stout thighs apart under
a big skirt   grandchild sliding
on   off my lap   a pleasant
summer perspiration

that's my old man across the yard
he's talking to the meter reader
he's telling him the world's sad story
how electricity is oil or uranium
and so forth   I tell my grandson
run over to your grandpa   ask him
to sit beside me for a minute   I
am suddenly exhausted by my desire
to kiss his sweet explaining lips

GRACE PALEY

Afterword

So you've figured out to kiss off the "everything everything everything" that kept you from being your true self. Now you're kissing the sky and the ground and the entire beautiful world because you've found your mojo again, you've learned to be happy. Still, don't be shocked if the old you, Ms. I'm All Alone and Hating It rears her miserable head. Like on a glorious fall day, when you're driving through the park with the radio on and the sun roof open—and suddenly a gargantuan SUV bears down on your tail and you feel that familiar surge of righteous rage. How dare this soccer mom with her car full of snot-nosed yuppie kids try to run you off the road? You have a right to be here too, even if it is just you and your Saturn on the way to get your hair highlighted. Why do you have to get out of *her* way, Ms. I've Got Everything You

Ever Wanted and Then Some? But you do, and as she speeds past, you flip her off, feel like a jerk, and find yourself back in a funk.

If it comes to that, then pick up this book. Find a poem to match that moment of fury and frustration, like Ethridge Knight's "Feeling Fucked Up." Go ahead and think, "Fuck music and clouds drifting in the sky . . . fuck/the whole mothafucking thing." And then remember to take a look at Stephen Crane's poem "The Heart." If you keep flipping off poor harried moms and their kids, it really will just be you and your highlights alone in your Saturn eating your bitter heart out. You know that's not who you want to be. You want to be the fulfilled grandmother with her "nicely mapped face," laughing in her garden in Grace Paley's poem "Here."

Obviously, just because you've found yourself and a sense of happiness again doesn't mean that you won't still experience moments and days of Hurting. No one can find an absolutely perfect way to live in this world—heartache and loss can always sneak up on us. And the stages that we describe in *Kiss Off* aren't absolutely perfect either.

If you read all of these poems straight through, you won't necessarily be healed for life. Just because you've made it to Believing doesn't mean you won't find yourself Reeling again someday.

But this time around you'll have the *Kiss Off* poems to keep you company, offer empathy, and cheer you on. Let "Sadie's Poem" get you fired up; laugh your way to a fresh perspective with "The Pope's Penis"; remember the glorious brilliance of grand responses to everyday events described in "We Take Our Children to Ireland."

We hope you take these poems to heart and use them as a source of strength and inspiration. They'll help you recognize what you're feeling and remind you of who you want to be—a true believer in herself, in life, and in love.

Biographies of Contributors

ANNA AKHMATOVA (1889–1966): Russian lyric poet whose work includes *Evening, Rosary, and White Flock*. She achieved great popular success in Russia for her work.

ELIZABETH ALEXANDER (1962–): Her collections of poems include *Antebellum Dream Book* and *Body of Life*. She has taught in many universities in the United States.

GUILLAUME APOLLINAIRE (1880–1918): He settled in Paris in 1898 where he worked as a journalist, playwright, and poet.

ELIZABETH BISHOP (1911–1979): Highly regarded American poet who won every major poetry award in the United States including the Pulitzer

Prize and the National Book Award, she served as Chancellor of the Academy of American Poets from 1966 until 1979.

STERLING A. BROWN (1901–1989): An influential American poet, he taught at Howard University. His first collection was *Southern Road*.

LUCILLE CLIFTON (1936–): Mentored by Sterling Brown at Howard University, she worked as an actor while writing poetry. She was nominated for a Pulitzer Prize in 1980 and won the National Book Award for Poetry in 2001 for *Blessing the Boats: New and Selected Poems, 1988–2000*.

JOHNNY COLEY (1950–): He was born in Alexander City, Alabama, and has published three chapbooks of poetry, *Good Luck, No*, and *Peasant Attitudes towards Art*.

BILLY COLLINS (1941–): According to the *New York Times*, Collins is currently the "most popular poet in America." He is currently the Poet Laureate of the United States.

STEPHEN CRANE (1871–1900): Best known for his novel *The Red Badge of Courage,* he published one volume of poetry. He died of tuberculosis at the age of twenty-nine.

CAROLYN CREEDON (1969–): Creedon's poems have been included in the Best American Poetry series. She currently works as a waitress in San Francisco.

EMILY DICKINSON (1830–1886): One of the nineteenth century's greatest poets, Dickinson lived quietly at home in Amherst, Massachusetts, with her lawyer father. Only seven of her approximately one thousand poems were published during her lifetime.

GREGORY DJANIKIAN (1949–): Originally from Alexandria, Egypt, he teaches at the University of Pennsylvania. His latest collection of poetry is called *Years Later.*

MARK DOTY (1953–): Contemporary American poet, he has won the National Book Critics Circle

Award and the T. S. Eliot Prize. His most recent collection is *Source*. He lives in New York City.

SHAWN M. DURRETT (1974–): Born and raised in the hills of western Massachusetts, Durrett received her MFA in poetry from the University of Michigan. Her poem "Lures," included here, won an Academy of American Poets Prize in 1998.

RICHARD EBERHART (1904–): Minnesota-born poet, he has received the Bollingen Prize, the Pulitzer Prize, and the National Book Award. He has taught at many universities in the United States.

DEBORAH GARRISON (1965–): Garrison published *A Working Girl Can't Win and Other Poems* in 1998. She lives in Montclair, New Jersey.

DAVID GEWANTER is the author of *In the Belly* (U. Chicago Press, 1997), *The Sleep of Reason* (U. Chicago Press, 2003), and coeditor with Frank Bidart of *The Collected Poems of Robert Lowell* (Farrar, Straus and Giroux, 2003).

Louise Glück (1943–): American poet whose collections have won both the Pulitzer Prize (1992) and the National Book Critics Circle Award (1985).

Robert Graves (1895–1985): British poet, novelist, and essayist, he was professor of poetry at Oxford from 1961 until 1966.

Lola Haskins (1943–): She has published six books of poetry. Her most recent work is *The Rim-Benders*.

Robert Hayden (1913–1980): His first volume of poems was *Heart-Shape in the Dust*; his last collection was *American Journal* (1978). He taught at Fisk University and the University of Michigan.

Robert Herrick (1591–1674): Considered to be one of the finest English lyric poets, he lived in London and Dean Prior, Devonshire.

Sadie Lisk Highsmith (1998–): Sadie currently attends ArtsTogether, a preschool in Raleigh, North Carolina.

JANE HIRSHFIELD (1953–): American poet who studied at the San Francisco Zen Center for eight years, she has translated several collections of Japanese poetry. Her works include *The October Palace*, *The Lives of the Heart*, and *Given Sugar, Given Salt*.

GERARD MANLEY HOPKINS (1844–1889): Although his poetry did not garner critical acclaim during his lifetime, he is now considered a major British poet.

LANGSTON HUGHES (1902–1967): The most important writer of the Harlem Renaissance, he published ten books of poetry, including *Montage of a Dream Deferred*. He lived in New York City.

JANE KENYON (1947–1995): She published four volumes of poetry, including *Constance* (1993). She lived at Eagle Pond Farm in New Hampshire until she died of leukemia in 1995.

GALWAY KINNELL (1927–): Kinnell has won both the National Book Award and the Pulitzer Prize for poetry.

ETHERIDGE KNIGHT (1931–1991): Knight began writing poetry while he was incarcerated at Indiana State Prison. His book *Poems from Prison* received great critical acclaim in the United States.

KIM KONOPKA lives in Santa Fe, New Mexico, where she writes and teaches poetry. Her work has won several awards and been extensively published.

PHILIP LARKIN (1922–1985): He was a highly influential British poet whose collections of poetry included *The Less Deceived* and *High Window*.

LYN LIFSHIN: Author of more than one hundred books, she has been Poet in Residence at the University of Rochester, Antioch, and Colorado Mountain College. Her most recent collection is *Before It's Light*.

ANDREW MARVELL (1621–1678): Known primarily as a satirist during his lifetime, he came to be considered a great poet only after his death.

CLAUDE MCKAY (1890–1948): His books include *Songs of Jamaica* and *Harlem Shadows*. He emigrated from Jamaica to the United States in 1912 and lived in New York City.

LYNNE MCMAHON (1951–): McMahon has published one collection of poetry, *The House of Entertaining Science*. She teaches at the University of Missouri.

JOHN MILTON (1608–1674): He was a scholar and theologian. *Paradise Lost* is considered one of the greatest works in the English language.

PABLO NERUDA (1904–1973): Nobel Prize–winning Chilean poet, he received the Lenin Peace Prize in 1953.

JOYCE CAROL OATES (1938–): Her most recent collection of poems is *The Time Traveler*. A prolific novelist, she currently teaches in the creative writing program at Princeton University.

FRANK O'HARA (1926–1966): O'Hara worked at

the Museum of Modern Art in New York City for most of his life. He published his first volume of poems, *A City in Winter and Other Poems,* in 1952, and over the course of his life, he published five more collections.

SHARON OLDS (1942–): Often described as a confessional poet, Olds won the National Book Critics Circle Award for *The Dead and the Living* in 1983.

HANS OSTROM (1954–): Ostrom is the author of *A Langston Hughes Encyclopedia.* A widely published poet, he teaches at the University of Puget Sound.

GRACE PALEY (1922–): Paley is best known as a short story writer, particularly for her collection *Enormous Changes at the Last Minute.* She lives in New York City and Vermont.

DOROTHY PARKER (1893–1967): She was a journalist, humorist, and a founding member of the famous Algonquin Round Table. Her collections of poetry include *Enough Rope, Sunset Gun,* and *Death and Taxes.*

LINDA PASTAN (1932–): Her collection *PM/AM: New and Selected Poems* was nominated for an American Book Award in 1983. She lives and works in Potomac, Maryland.

MARGE PIERCY (1936–): Novelist and poet, Piercy has published eleven collections of poetry. She lives on Cape Cod.

MARIE PONSOT (1921–): Author of several collections of poetry, her recent work includes *The Bird Catcher,* for which she won the National Book Critics Circle Award for poetry. Her latest collection of poems is *Springing: New and Selected Poems.* She teaches at Columbia University and lives in New York City.

WILLIAM SHAKESPEARE (1564–1616): Believed by many to be the greatest writer in the English language, he acted, lived, and wrote in London and Stratford-upon-Avon.

WALLACE STEVENS (1879–1955): He was a poet and insurance executive in Hartford, Connecticut.

His collections of poetry include *Harmonium* and *Collected Poems*.

ANNA SWIRSZCZYNSKA (1909–1984): Swir, as she is known in English publications, was a Polish poet and playwright. She lived in Kraków until her death in 1984.

WISLAWA SZYMBORSKA (1923–): Nobel prize-winning Polish poet, she lives in Kraków. Her work includes *Sounds, Feelings, Thoughts: Seventy Poems*.

ELIZABETH ASH VÉLEZ (1945–): Journalist and writer, Vélez teaches at Georgetown University.

LARRY VÉLEZ (1945–): Writer and poet, he currently lives and works in Washington, D.C.

VIRGIL (70 B.C.–19 B.C.): Hailed as the greatest Roman poet, Virgil is best known for his epic *The Aeneid*.

DEREK WALCOTT (1930–): He is a Saint Lucian poet and playwright who won the Nobel Prize for literature in 1992. His collections of poems include *Sea Grapes* and *In a Green Night*.

WANG WEI (699–759): Chinese poet, painter, and musician, he was the founder of southern Chinese landscape art. His poems were translated in 1959 by Chang Yin-nan and L. C. Walmsley.

WILLIAM CARLOS WILLIAMS (1883–1963): Winner of both the National Book Award and the Pulitzer Prize, Williams practiced medicine in Rutherford, New Jersey. His collections include *Journey to Love* and *The Broken Span*.

JAMES WRIGHT (1927–1980): He was a highly regarded American poet who won the Pulitzer Prize in 1966. His work includes *To a Blossoming Pear Tree* and *This Journey*.

WILLIAM BUTLER YEATS (1865–1939): Considered the greatest of Irish poets, he received the Nobel Prize for literature in 1923.

Acknowledgments

Special thanks to our amazing agent, Miriam Altshuler, and her assistant, Sara McGhee, our wonderful editor, Molly Chehak, our indefatigable publicist, Tina Andreadis, and our friend Andrew Carroll of the American Poetry and Literacy Project.

We also want to thank our friends at Georgetown University and WETA Public Television and Radio: Leona Fisher, Patricia O'Connor, Norma Tilden, Joe Sitterson, Dennis Williams, and Zoe Kalendek Lukas; and Maura Daly Phinney, Erika Robinson, Kate Hawley, Thanh Bui, Janet Riksen, Fran Planning, DeLinda Mrowka, Suzanne Masri, and Andrea Murray.

Thanks also to Ken and Sandy Roberts and their friends. Special thanks to Jean Ash, Renee Blaloch, Susan Lisk, Barbara Lanphier, Richard

Appel, Mary Hutchins, Colleen O'Conner, Linda Kramer, and Ericka Souter, Matt Klam, the Hotel George, all the Cliffords, especially Garry, Pross Gifford and Jennifer Rutland from the Library of Congress, Poets House, the New York Public Library, Politics and Prose bookstore, and Fred Courtwright.

Elizabeth gratefully acknowledges the love, support, and gorgeous, brilliant shite of husband Larry and sons Stephen and Nicholas. And Mary thanks her husband, Greg, for happiness and wedded bliss and everything everything everything.

About the Editors

MARY D. ESSELMAN is a teacher and writer. She lives with her husband in Washington, D.C.

ELIZABETH ASH VÉLEZ is director of the Community Scholars Program at Georgetown University, where she also teaches women's studies and nonfiction writing.